How I Made Lemonade

ANGIE MANSEY

How I Made Lemonade: A Memoir
© Angie Mansey 2021

ISBN: 978-1-922461-84-1 (Paperback)
         978-1-922461-85-8 (eBook)

 A catalogue record for this book is available from the National Library of Australia

NATIONAL LIBRARY OF AUSTRALIA

Lead Editor: Kristy Martin
Editor: Jason Martin
Original Cover Photo: Renae Soppe-Bryan, Sunshine Coast Pinup School
Cover Design: Ocean Reeve Publishing
Design and Typeset: Ocean Reeve Publishing
Printed in Australia by Ocean Reeve Publishing

Published by Angie Mansey and Ocean Reeve Publishing
www.oceanreevepublishing.com

OCEAN REEVE PUBLISHING

Sometimes it is the very people who no one imagines anything of, who do the things that no one can imagine.

—ALAN TURING

DEDICATION

To my husband, who loved me before I knew how to love myself and saw the woman I was going to become on that first day of high school. Thank you for being my true love. This is all for you. I am forever yours.

To R. You were the reason I kept going. You gave me the greatest role of my life, and everything I am is due to you alone. I am so proud of you, and I love you dearly. Don't get red on you.

To my sons: R, C, D, and A. Being your mother is a privilege and an honour that I am immensely proud of. You are the most magical and pure loves of my life. I believe in you. Stand up, be proud of yourselves, and live life like you are the brightest shooting star in the sky. I will forever be cheering you on by your side. Also, please skip chapter four.

To the friends who have become the family that I never had: thank you for laughing, crying, and celebrating life with me. Your presence means more than you know. Do epic shit.

To the doctors and nurses who have been the reason I was even able to bring my son home: I will forever be indebted to you; thank you for being selfless and incredible humans. The nurses, doctors, and staff in 6B at Princess Margaret Hospital: you are the reason I still have my son; thank you for keeping him going and teaching me how to nurse him. You truly are superheroes.

For L.J. You will never be forgotten. Forever young.

To the person who told me, 'Careful about sticking your neck out by starting a charity and continuing to be in the public eye, because people like you who have skeletons in their closet will likely get it cut off.' Checkmate.

CONTENTS

PREFACE

In a world of smoke and mirrors and flattering filters, I have decided that I would be brave and let people know what has happened behind the spotlight: the things that have made me the successful woman I am today. I am writing this knowing that people will judge me— harshly, I am sure—and I am okay with that. I also write in fear of finally speaking out about what I hid in shame for years: homelessness, domestic violence, miscarriage, and divorce.

I am at a point in my life where showing people the highlight reel would be a false interpretation of how I got to be where I am now. I have fallen plenty of times, but I always got up again.

I want people to know that you don't have to be perfect or come from a privileged background to leave your mark on the world. Others' opinions or bad genetics don't define you. Past behaviour doesn't always sum up who you are, and even if you aren't the most educated person in the room, you can always be the hardest-working and the kindest.

As I stand now, I am a proudly self-made businesswoman. I own and run my own business, and I am the founder and director of a charity that gives financial support to families of terminally ill children in my community. I have won multiple business and community awards, spoken on stages, received standing ovations for speeches and accolades, and been on television and in magazines countless times. I have four wonderful sons, and I am married to my best friend. But that, my friends, is purely the highlight reel.

So how did this girl who was involuntarily admitted into an adult psychiatric unit at age fourteen, slept in school bag racks, dropped out of high school, became pregnant at sixteen, and escaped an abusive relationship go on to rebuild her life?

Well, I will give you a hint. There isn't just one plot twist, there are a few, and they are really good, but better than that, they are real. This story is about what it took for me to be who I am today. I am ashamed of some parts, proud of others, but honest about it all. Oscar Wilde once said, 'We are all in the gutter, but some of us are looking at the stars.'

Well, I am the girl who looked at the stars.

Angie Mansey

CHAPTER 1

SMELLS LIKE TEEN SPIRIT

As a young girl, I was so unremarkable that if someone had been forced to reference my existence in a book and accidentally smudged the wet ink of my name, removing all trace, not a soul would have noticed. I had a remarkably uneventful blue-collar upbringing filled with all the average extracurricular activities—such as swimming, dance, and sports—typical of a childhood of the 1980s and 1990s.

I grew up in a small beachside town called Caloundra on the Sunshine Coast, back when it was safe to stay out late until the streetlights came on. There were four television channels, and local phone numbers had only six digits.

I was to be in the graduating class of 2000, which meant 1996 was the year it all kicked off. For those not around then, or those wanting a nice trip down memory lane, it was the generation of wearing poorly-matched Revlon ColorStay® foundation and Impulse® body spray. Offspring was about to release *Americana*, and No Doubt's 'Just a Girl' was played on repeat on mainstream radio stations. The guys at school seemed to smell of Lynx® Africa collectively, and Adidas® snap pants were a thing. Simple®'s brand of skate shoes had just made an appearance, and *Romeo + Juliet* was freshly released at the cinemas.

I started high school almost invisible, with skin so pale that the nickname 'Casper the ghost' was given to me within days. I rocked a pretty epic head of dark blonde curls that refused to be tamed and were often held in place with a ponytail and hairspray. I wore knock-off Dr Martens® (as the real thing was certainly not in the family budget) and a yellow and blue plastic Bananas in Pyjamas® watch on my left hand. My light green eyes had a passion for reading, and I had a tiny athletic frame from years of dance and sports, but nothing about me would in any way give a clue to my insane life that was to come.

I was a fairly average student, not excelling in any area in particular, with the constant feedback that 'Angela would greatly improve her grades if she paid more attention in class and wasn't so easily distracted'. I stumbled through maths, which would continue into my high school years. Even with the help of a private tutor and extra classes, I failed dismally and could never quite get my head around fractions, long division, and, even worse, algebra. Although everyone insisted I would desperately need these skills in my future, I have yet to find a use for an improper fraction at any point in my professional career.

However, I could never get enough of reading. I could devour an entire novel in twenty-four hours, and during my younger years, I would be a constant fixture at the local library. I would take any moment I had to immerse myself into other worlds and the lives of people who I considered to be extraordinary and fascinating. My love of the written word was so sincere that well after bedtime, I could be found huddled under the blankets with the bedside lamp glowing, trying to sneak in another chapter. My parentals resolved this swiftly by the removal of said lamp, followed by the removal of the torch I had begun to use as a substitute. Finally, I realised that if I sat at the correct angle at the end of my bed and tilted my blinds in the right direction, the street light on the curb gave just enough radiance to assist my nocturnal pursuits of escapism. There were only two books in our household growing up. Both were owned by my father and written by Dale Carnegie. I must have read them cover to cover by the age of nine, and to this day, I still have his books among my now-vast collection.

I excelled in sports and dance and received As in any class that had physical movement or health involved. I remember having my first and last feminist moment in Grade 8 when forced to do a sewing and cooking class. I announced I would not need this skill as I wasn't going to have children and was going to be a highly paid executive of some description. Ah, the irony of it all.

I was dedicated to my dancing and karate; I won the State Championships in my karate division when I was thirteen, had multiple dancing trophies, and made the regional school sports teams each year in various events. I was kind, courteous, and disciplined until those traits were the least defining qualities that I became known for.

I am not sure if even a soap opera could make the storyline of my life believable. The plot twists are crazy, the characters are almost surreal at best, and the highs and lows would make even the most bipolar temperament seem tame.

By the time the Passion Pop® had run out in my tenth year at school, I had successfully burned every bridge close to me, and even that would be saying it mildly. To say I lit them with sticks of dynamite while stomping in the tatters of the reputation that I had earned while thrusting one finger crudely in the air would be a more accurate description.

I can't quite pinpoint what it was that suddenly flicked inside of me, but the foundation of the path of my rebellious destruction was laid in the summer of 1997. I was mid-way through my second year at high school when I started to find my voice. I had been pretty timid up until that point, staying close to my circle of friends who I grew up with in primary school. I didn't have an overly unhappy childhood although, growing up, I had this unshakeable feeling that I didn't belong. There was a distance that I could never quite close between my parents and a looming sense of tension that I could never shake.

The mood at home always had a strange feeling of awkwardness, as though my family was putting on a front and playing the roles of happy husband, wife, and daughter. I cannot recall a moment growing up where there was a simple act of affection shown between my mother and father. I saw plenty of unhealthy coping mechanisms, and felt the tension that would sweep across the room before a door was slammed or a snide comment made. The communication between them was sparse at best. Jarring digs were spoken, and unappreciated gifts were given with open disdain, as though to prove that no amount of effort could break down a barrier that had been set in stone years earlier.

I didn't ever experience that important mother-daughter bond that is often spoken about. In fact, from an early age, the constant emotion of being too separated, too disconnected, too different, and generally just too much was very real for me. I can recall the humiliating accusation of being a self-centred and vain teenager due to the time I spent in front of the bathroom mirror.

The words rang embarrassingly in my ears as I tried to defend myself by explaining that I was self-conscious and I was attempting to make myself look pretty before facing the day. I can never remember being told I was beautiful or smart or, as a young girl, having any positive affirmations reinforced—my insecurity as I grew started to show. I distinctly recall being told, 'I pity the man that ends up marrying you' in the middle of family disagreements, as though my inability to agree with the status quo was going to be a downfall. It also implied that, in some way, my ability to find a husband was something that would prove my worth as a person.

I didn't have much in common with my tiny family, and as the only athletic blonde in a family of brunettes, my physical differences weren't the only obvious separation.

I had aspirations, dreams of wanting satisfaction in life and a genuine belief in the far-flung notion of a soulmate who I could build these dreams with. I was a romantic at heart, most likely evolving from my primary school years devouring Enid Blyton and Jackie Collins novels.

I dreamed of a life so far removed from the existence I was born into that I would continually tell my parents I was leaving home the moment I finished school. I couldn't wait to make my way in the world. I never knew just how quickly this would come around and how it would unfold. I would often find my escape in my friends or my boyfriends, and their families would become the support people I needed to get me through those early years.

My best friends since primary school were Amy and Sam. I spent time at Amy's house whenever possible, and we shared all our secrets together as young girls do. She was there when I discovered a rather big underlying secret that seemed to sit just beneath the surface inside my household. It happened quite innocently and rather by accident one afternoon. Amy and I were doing craft projects for our high school drama class and had run out of staples. We headed into the garage to get to the filing cabinet and searched the drawers. I came across a closed container in the bottom. I opened it and was totally unprepared for what was inside. I held it out to Amy, who just stared at me in shock. 'That's drugs, Ang!'

I shook my head. 'No way ...' We quickly closed the container and put everything back as we found it, disappearing back into my bedroom to discuss what we had found and swear each other to secrecy about our discovery.

I held onto my newfound knowledge for a couple of weeks before I approached my mother about what I had found. Her lack of shock over it was probably the most alarming revelation I had. It clearly wasn't hers, and she expressed that she didn't agree and appeared mortified I had found out that my father had a substance abuse issue. I made her promise she wouldn't tell him I knew. I didn't want to get into trouble for telling on him. But within days, the awkward tension that swept the house made it clear that he was aware I had found his secret and broken his trust by speaking out about it. I was truly confused as I would never have suspected anything; it was never spoken about again. This was the very first of a long line of substance abuse secrets that I discovered hidden in our family. I really learnt then the meaning of a quote, 'What you permit, you promote; what you allow, you encourage; what you condone, you own.' It was permitted in our household, and it wasn't spoken about. It took me many years to stop that continual generational allowance to things that I do not condone in my household.

I pretended it never happened and moved on with all the exciting things that happen when you are a young girl, like fall in love for the first time. My first real boyfriend was Luke. He wore baggy pants with his boxer shorts showing at the waist, crisp white Nike® t-shirts and had braids in his long blonde hair, which was continuously covered with a basketball cap. We had met on the first day of high school at our very first class of the day, English. We became instant friends. He pursued me for well over a year until I let my guard down and then, of course, fell head over heels in love.

Typically for the era, we had our first kiss at a blue light disco to some corny Backstreet Boys song; I could never recall the name. Soon after, we declared we were destined to be together forever. We would spend our weekends watching *Video Hits* music clips in my lounge room and taking his small tinny boat out on the local waterways to explore the small islands a few kilometres from home.

I had my first alcoholic drink sitting cross-legged on the carpeted floor of my bedroom with him; I was given a couple of West Coast wine coolers, and he had some cheap version of bourbon from my parent's pantry. We sat there giggling to ourselves, thinking we were incredibly mature as we listened to the Top 40 music countdown on my radio and made mixtapes. Luke was romantic and sweet, the type of boyfriend who left a trail of roses to my bedroom while he hid in my wardrobe as the latest Hanson song, 'I Will Come to You', played on the second-hand stereo on my dresser.

Luke wrote songs about me and gave me love letters every lunch break. He ended up living with my family for a few weeks while his parents were away for work and instantly became part of the furniture. He had the most beautiful blue eyes that I had ever seen and our school diaries and pencil cases became proudly emblazoned with each other's initials.

We were infatuated, as first loves tend to be, and on our four-month anniversary exchanged gold promise rings with each other. Luke's was a thick gold wedding band that he wore proudly on his right hand with the words 'Forever Yours' engraved on the inside, and I wore a diamond and gold forget-me-not ring to seal our devotion to one another.

It was all adorable and innocent, but I was very young and started to feel a little claustrophobic from all of the serious attention and heartfelt declarations of love. As first loves often go, heartbreak was to follow. As I stared down at a packet of contraceptive pills that my mother had taken me to a family planning clinic to receive, I felt trapped and in way over my head. I had no real understanding of how to handle a mature relationship. I had no older role model in my household that I could openly discuss such personal matters with, and I followed an example that I frequently saw around my home and closed my emotions down, pulling myself away.

Although I felt terrible for breaking his heart, I ended our high school romance as swiftly as it began. It took some time for us to find our feet as 'just friends' again, I knew I had caused him pain, and I was guilt-ridden by it for a long time.

We broke up just before school finished in the summer in 1997, and I spent the holidays growing into a young woman, changing both personally and physically, becoming a bolder, more mature version of the little girl I was before.

Trying hard to look like a surfer chick now became my ambition. Growing up by the beach meant every spare moment that year was spent covered in baby oil and tanning in bikinis with friends while watching the older boys surf and trying to get their attention by not-so-subtly giggling in their direction and prancing in the shallows.

While it didn't win me any points for originality, it *did* win me a new romance with a bronzed-skinned and blonde-haired surfer called Joel. Joel had a charismatic charm about him and a cheeky smile that lit up the room. Joel lived nearby but attended a private school, where he was about to enter his final year as a celebrated rugby player and general all-round popular sportsman.

Joel would ride his retro cruiser bike fresh from his morning surf to my house every morning, and then he would double me on his handlebars to whatever adventure we were going on that day. I thought he was incredible; he made my heart race, and I would instantly get butterflies every time I saw him riding down the path leading into my quiet cul-de-sac.

In the small court where I lived, all the families knew each other, and I grew particularly close with our immediate next-door neighbours; they were a couple of years younger than my parents and had three small children who I would help babysit at times.

Janette, or Jen as she was affectionately known, quickly became a strong mother figure in my life. She was someone I looked up to and would often spend evenings watching television with and confiding to while her husband worked long shifts as a police officer.

My relationship with my own mother had always been temperamental, and my refuge was often to escape next door and seek advice from Jen. I had known her since I was eleven; our families became friends the moment they moved in beside us. We had spent the last couple of years all taking family holidays together, and that New Year's was no exception.

This particular year's destination was Sawtell, a coastal village in northern New South Wales, with plans to celebrate with Jen's extended family over the festive season. Joel had a part-time job, which meant he was unable to travel down with us. So I headed down in Jen's car with a small convoy of cars and camper trailers following close behind.

I had become close friends with her nephew, Danny, who was my age, and his younger sister, Tammy. We had known each other for the past two years. Each school holidays would see them travel up to Jen's house or she would venture down, taking me with her for the road trip. These adventures were the highlight of my year as we all got along so well and looked forward to catching up at every opportunity. Danny and I had a cute friendship that only ever crossed over once in those years, with a stolen kiss one evening while we sat on the big brick letterbox that marked his home.

I am not sure if it was something in the air during that hot New Year's Eve but the lives of those who sat around the bonfire that evening would end the year in a very different manner from how they started. Within twelve months of that night, the four married couples—Jen and her husband, my parents, Danny's parents, and even their neighbours who joined the celebrations—would all be divorced, separated across all parts of the country. We would never share another family holiday again.

I don't remember how it came to be, but even on that holiday, I stayed with Danny's family instead of mine. Anything to avoid the tension that was bubbling to the surface within my own family unit.

I returned from our holiday down south to find myself quickly bundled off to my grandparents in New Zealand for another week before returning for the last couple of the summer holidays. Looking back, I can only imagine that that was some kind of last-ditch effort from my parents to see if they had a relationship that could be saved. But at the time, I tried to ignore the uncomfortable feeling that I had become accustomed to.

My mother had a sister who also lived in New Zealand, although the relationship between the two certainly wasn't a close one. My father was estranged from his family, so there were no other family members involved: no aunts, uncles, cousins, or family get-togethers. Looking back, it was a strange, isolating childhood, but back then, I really didn't know any better.

After the summer holidays were over, I found myself walking back into Caloundra High School's Year 10 class with sun-bleached blonde hair, a dark tan, a much shorter skirt, a surfer boyfriend, and

9

plenty of attitude. The cheap Dr Marten® knock-offs and plastic watch were nowhere to be seen. My newfound confidence took a pretty big hit only a few weeks later, however, when I walked home from school and, upon reaching my driveway, found my father in a state of devastation, putting a suitcase into the boot of his car. He managed to explain my mother had asked him to leave and that she wanted a divorce. I stood shell-shocked at what was unfolding and watched heartbroken as he drove away with his shoulders heaving in sobs.

This, while appearing to have come straight out of left field, had been hinted at for years when late-night arguments filtered through my bedroom walls. I never really imagined my parents following through with it. Their relationship was always fractured, and I always presumed this was the normal way we were going to continue to function; I didn't think it would ever stop.

I had the most in common with Dad. When the tensions and the hysteria inside the home became almost unbearable, he had a way of making make me feel that I could withstand it and that he was on my side and together we could get through anything. When he packed up and left that day, I assumed—like other children whose families had separated—that he would find a house close by and that I would find safety in building a new family home with him. But that never happened.

If you looked up the definition of 'bitter divorce', I have no doubt my parent's separation would tick all the boxes as the prime example. Both hurting and unable to find a way to communicate with each other, it was destined to blow up badly. I just thought they would stay together, or at the very least become amicable, but that day was a catalyst for a change I never saw coming.

The most devastating action I remember from this time was crying to my mum about how upset I was with Dad, and that I felt so hurt, let down, and sad. Somehow this ended with fourteen-year-old me writing a letter that consisted of every single slight that I felt my father had done to me over the years, an overwhelming emotional pouring of accusations and hurt on paper. A phone call was made, and he was asked to return to the family home that he had been asked to leave only weeks earlier and told to sit on the lounge as I was encouraged to read each word of that letter to an already broken man, so he knew how I felt. To this day, I have no idea why someone would allow that to happen. It wasn't my decision to do that, and I was torn between anger in every direction. I was too young to comprehend I was possibly being used to break down a person further beyond repair. It must have just about killed him, and my heart still aches at the thought of this scene being played out. I must have blocked it from my memory as it wasn't until many years later that my father had to remind me of this evening and how it tore him apart. The cruelty behind it was shattering.

Within a few short months, my father had decided to leave Queensland entirely as the weight of the divorce loomed heavily over us all. He knew some old friends from New Zealand who had moved to Western Australia years prior and declared that he was going to start a new life over there. The pain was too much to bear, staying here with the family in tatters. He made sure to give me his contact number and promised to be in touch regularly. Then he left, a shadow of the man he used to be.

Somehow, in the middle of it all, the family home was sold in a hurry and at a loss. My mother wasn't working and needed the cash for us to survive. With cars and possessions also being sold, we managed to lose what felt like everything all at once. It was a depressing time, and trying to keep finding positives was proving extremely hard for me. I contracted a severe case of whooping cough. I remember having an old neighbour take me in and nurse me whilst our belongings were moved into the new unit. I moved with my mother from the bright, big family home into a small rental unit that had an atmosphere as dark as the horrid bricks that lined the walls. My bed didn't hold up in the move, and without the funds available to buy another, initially, I had a mattress on the floor and scarf-like sarongs used as curtains while I tried to find my way in this new life.

With my dad gone and communication sporadic as he tried to

find his feet again, I felt lost and abandoned with my mother. We had struggled at the best of times to understand one another and having my father taken out of the equation just elevated the apparent divide between us. I had lost the person who stepped in and kept everything on track when the household started to get slightly skewed. I had also lost the person who I could turn to for advice.

My dad was by no means the perfect father or role model, but he was an exceptional man who did the absolute best he could. With the knowledge he had, he gave me the tools to have a better life than he did. My dad grew up in a home filled with violence and neglect, and although he didn't have a role model to show him how to be a good parent, he was fair and tried his best. He was a straight-talking man who was more comfortable being alone than in a crowd, a little rough around the edges and with a temper that you would be best to avoid triggering with childish sarcasm or poor manners. He was known to hang up the family phone without a word if a friend called and didn't use their manners when asking for me. He demanded respect and had an old-fashioned sense of the world that I am proud to have inherited. He would often tell me to 'do as I say and not as I do' and would at times, when I caught him in the right moments, tell me about the horrors of his times growing up. He would say it in such a nonchalant way and reiterate how it didn't define who he was and, in turn, would show me how both of my parents' behaviours also didn't define who I was.

In the uncertain time that I found myself in I decided to cling to Joel, his lifestyle, and friends; this meant an introduction to a new circle of friends, house parties, night-time surfing expeditions, and some wild nights making incredible memories. I spent the rest of that summer cruising the coast in our friend's old EH Holden® with the windows down, smoking Longbeach® Blue cigarettes, and feeling untouchable if I had Joel by my side. I didn't fit in at my new home situation and was trying to find my place in the world.

I was angry; I didn't want to be in these circumstances. As much as every teenager complains about their parents, it felt dreadful not having my dad with me. I felt torn between what at the time seemed to be choosing sides in this horrible situation. I felt for both of my parents, but the guilt I endured from watching my dad no longer be part of the family unit was soul-crushing. I wanted to hate them both, and I did, but I hated what was happening around me more. I knew they couldn't control each other's actions, and their own suffering was obvious, but it seemed incredibly unfair to me at the time.

I started to experience panic attacks and anxiety, which was very swiftly treated under doctor's instructions with an array of medications; anti-anxiety tablets, antidepressants, and mild sedative pills to take if I felt a panic attack come on. It was impressive I could still feel anything at all, as I was left mainly feeling like a zombie.

Shortly after, sleeping tablets were prescribed to assist my nocturnal nature. Regular therapy sessions with a psychiatrist were added to the regime of what I referred to as 'crazy management'. So began the meltdown that led to a chain of events that changed my life forever. By this stage, I was barely able to function properly, let alone think straight, and now I felt like an absolute failure, as though I couldn't even manage to make it through the age of fourteen without needing such full-on intervention. I stopped my sports, karate, and dance and spent my spare time being taken to new doctors to treat all these issues that I was mortified to be diagnosed with. Medicate, medicate, medicate; I had more pills in me than a junkie, and if I tried to take myself off them, which I did at times, the comedown was horrendous, and I would feel ill.

It was believed that if I followed what the doctor had prescribed, I would soon feel better. Only I didn't; I felt worse. I didn't want to take this ridiculous concoction that made me feel like I was almost comatose. I didn't want to be medicated, but I didn't want to not be coping. Whether or not there were other treatment options remained irrelevant, I was too busy trying to hide what was happening at home—and the medication I was taking—to reach out for help in other areas, and too young to know any better.

I stopped being able to keep up at school; the medication

made it hard to concentrate, and a side effect was feeling tired all the time. I started to sign out at lunchtime with the older, graduating class, and slowly my friendship circle began to change from those I grew up with to a new crowd. With them, I felt both invincible and lost at the same time, but most of the time, more than anything, I just felt alone. So, I filled that void, mainly with an angry attitude that tried to hide my pain and immature behaviour, but for the most part, it was innocent teenage fun-filled adventures while I tried to escape from myself and the reality of my life. I had no-one left to guide me, and I felt so insecure about my future that I did anything I could to be accepted into the small world of older friends that surrounded me.

I soon went from being the girl who was too scared to stand in front of the class and do an oral presentation to an extremely confident—almost to the point of an obnoxious—young lady. I think this was very much a front for the real emotions that bubbled under the surface. I felt so inferior and unworthy that I changed my personality to convince myself and those around me that I was okay, not hurting, and defiantly independent.

At this stage, the school stepped in due to my frequent absences. The medication had made my social anxiety increase instead of settling it. It was taking so much effort to put on such a strong front and fight through the anxiety and attend classes that on some days, it was just too much, and I wasn't able to go.

I was appointed a school counsellor I would have weekly meetings with. I continued to express how much I desperately hated being medicated, and that the doses or the type of medication I was being given had to be wrong, as I was barely functioning. What had started as quite normal teenage emotions of nerves and lacking in confidence were now evolving into a full-blown psychiatric condition. I was still trying to insist to everyone that it wasn't the case, that it has been blown out of proportion by the cycle of drugs I was prescribed. The drugs only seemed to make everything much worse.

While the school counsellor empathised, he was caught between my mother and my medical team. He was only able to assist me in being able to manage my class schedule in my drug-induced state. My regular classes were changed, and before I knew it, I was suddenly put in the 'high risk of dropping out' grouping. I had to take classes that prepared me to leave school and find employment. I was deemed highly likely to fail and the school set in motion what they thought would assist me in the next step of my life.

I couldn't have been more furious; clearly, this was all my own doing as I was unable to keep up with the workload, but in my mind, they were just another group of people who had no faith in me and what I was capable of achieving.

My options were thinning, and I was offered a traineeship at a small doughnut shop in the local shopping plaza. I can still recall my confusion as that was not in my career plan. *Didn't everyone see how much potential I had?* I am not sure what on earth I had expected to have happened, it was as if I was waiting for my invitation to university and couldn't see that I had not even remotely done the work that would allow me the opportunity to get there.

In my mind, I was going to be someone incredible and working in a doughnut shop wasn't going to get me where I needed to go. Lord only knows where my great ambition and drive to become someone who would make an impact on the world had gone. The levels of medication and the hours spent in front of various psychiatrists had dulled my ability to be capable of the smallest accomplishments. Only a few years prior, I was sure I was going to become a lawyer or a journalist, and now here I sat in a mess of my own making with very few choices left.

All this medication didn't slow my partying or my social life, which most certainly sped up a reputation that I was beginning to get in the small beachside town where I lived. But even that didn't seem to affect my choices. I did anything I could to prevent having to return home every evening into a house where I didn't feel welcome. I had successfully alienated all my school friends. They had no idea what was happening, and I was too ashamed to tell anyone about all the medication and therapist visits I was enduring, so I pushed anyone close as far away as possible.

The only person who knew the extent of all the events unfolding was Joel. We barely left each other's side, and my co-dependence on him was sky-high. I was an overemotional teenager in distress in a relationship that was filled with those highly charged emotions. The kind where each of you feels as though you would surely die if you weren't breathing the same air as each other. It was a dramatic and over-the-top existence we had created for ourselves.

It was the kind of relationship where we dreamed up names for our future children ('Reef' for a son, if I remember correctly). We daydreamed how we would live next to the beach to listen to the waves every morning, and we spent every moment by each other's side. We would sit on the beach and stare at the stars together as the waves rolled in. He spoke about running away to New Zealand when I turned sixteen, where we would get married, then we could come back home and find a place together. We would live happily ever after. I loved Joel dearly; I also knew that deep down he didn't love me like I had romanticised him to.

I was going through a world of hell, and the poor guy had to deal with my now-chaotic life. I know that I continually pushed him away, scared that my inability to be loved permanently was like a scar unable to be healed. I frequently started crossing boundaries to test his stead-fastness. I badly needed to have stability, and I expected something that wasn't even a remote possibility. I just wanted someone to save me, to make me part of a family again, to know that my existence mattered enough that someone would stay with me. My mother and father had been still battling out the terms of the divorce, money, and child support; there were constant attempts from her to get in touch with him from what I can recall at this stage. But he was not willing to talk with her, he had pulled right away from the conflict, and it seemed to only add to the atmosphere of frustration and helplessness in the unit.

After about a year together, Joel was to witness one of the most significant blows in my entire life. It all started as a typical weekend at my home, where we had settled ourselves in for a few drinks and some movies. Mixing drinks with the cocktail of medication I was being given was always going to be a recipe for disaster. I don't recall the play-by-play of what happened earlier that evening. All I remember was that Joel and I were alone in the house, the edges of my memory blurred by the haze of cheap wine and our deep and meaningful conversation somehow took a turn. I recall dissolving into tears over what I am sure was something minor but I had at some stage become inconsolable and acted out in the full throes of teenage angst. I must at some point have taken myself to the bathroom and, in an attention seeking moment of despair, made superficial cuts across my wrists with a blade of a broken disposable shaver. I know that Joel held me and assured me that everything was going to be okay, that we would make it through the hard times together, and I fell asleep in his arms on my bed. From all the moments of that evening that are clouded by intoxication, the moment I was awoken from my sleep by Jen's husband in his police uniform is crystal clear.

I remember being confused as he tried to explain I needed to come with him to hospital. I can recall telling him to stop joking and kept trying to roll over, but he persisted, and the look in his eyes was a mixture of sadness and concern. He lifted a sarong that I had hung on my window as a makeshift curtain and indicated to the patrol car waiting for me. He explained how the police had been called as I had been deemed a suicide risk, and he had come to take me in himself to try to lessen the blow of what was to come.

I was bewildered, and genuinely insisted that I was fine, and when they pointed out the superficial cuts I had made on my wrists, I pleaded they were just for attention. They were meagre scratches, nothing that even drew blood and indeed not anything that required even a hospital dressing of any kind. I couldn't find Joel anywhere; he had been sleeping right next to me when we went to bed and apparently got moved before they woke me, so as not to intervene.

Another police officer had come in at this stage, and I knew they were serious; they helped me pack a bag, continuing to reassure me that it was going to be okay.

As I left the unit, I looked back into the kitchen. I saw my kitchen table was surrounded by a group of my old neighbours who had all arrived at some ridiculously early hour of the morning to support my mother. My humiliation rose. With not an ounce of dignity left, I accepted what was about to happen and made my way to the hospital in the back of the police car.

On the way, I was told I was being escorted to the psychiatric ward. Calls had been made to arrange my admission; it was involuntary on my behalf, as a minor, and I had no power to change the situation. I was heartbroken, petrified, and devastated. I had never been so terrified of anything in my life. I don't know what services were available back then to assist in situations like this. Still, the decision was made, and I was locked up in the adult psychiatric ward as a terrified fourteen-year-old who now felt she was alone in the world.

I knew I wasn't crazy or suicidal; I was a frustrated and rebellious teenager who didn't know how to gain control of my situation. I had desperately wanted to stop taking all the heavy dosages of medication for some time, but when you are young, you don't have many options. It is having options that gives you control over your life. I was underage, so I had no voice at all. The police officer had apologised profusely and had personally tried to help me save face and support me. I will forever be grateful for him being there during that time. He didn't want to be shepherding me off to the psych ward, and he tried his best to reassure me as he led me through the heavily secured set of double doors at the ward.

The first thing they did was to search me and my bags in case I had anything I could use to harm myself. I remember being frozen in fear and, with tears in my eyes, kept insisting I didn't belong there. I desperately wanted someone to see through what this giant mess was and see who I was; *why couldn't anyone instantly recognise that I didn't belong here?* The medication was again rolled out, and I was escorted into a vacant, isolated, beige and grey bedroom with a single bed and a small bedside table that held my small toiletry bag. I noticed, later on, they'd removed my razor during the admissions search. Aside from a large window in my locked door, the room was devoid of any personality or embellishments. The lights were controlled on a tight schedule (as was everything inside the unit) and I was to be woken by a bright fluorescent glow every morning. I was shown to the bathroom and broke down in tears as I realised the nurse following me through the door was there to watch as I went to the toilet. I had never experienced anything like that before and felt so degraded and low.

I found the chair in the most solitary corner of the ward's open-plan day room, and with my arms hugging my knees, I sat in fear watching everything unfold around me. People were stumbling around me in various states of distress, mumbling incoherently, or yelling at empty spaces, their minds filled with whatever they imagined. I was too scared to move; I didn't want to eat and barely said a word when other patients rambled incomprehensible words in my direction. A nurse took sympathy on me, delivering a Vegemite® sandwich to me at some point after I had been too overwhelmed to join the line of adults at mealtime. I held on to a tiny Elmo® doll Jen had given me on my fourteenth birthday, and I felt my whole body try to disappear into itself as the distress of the circumstances washed over me.

The days inside passed like pure hell, with therapists analysing me, my situation, and my home life at length. I interacted with various teams of doctors and spent many hours talking with them, going over the medication I had been previously prescribed, the concerns that had been expressed in order to get my initial lockdown, and what the big picture was. I knew I was trapped. I couldn't leave; the law stated that a legal guardian had to sign official paperwork to allow that to happen, and I only had one in the state of Queensland at the time. It was the same person who had made the arrangements and signed me in: my mother.

I had my suspicions at the time that somebody called a friend of my father's over in Western Australia in an attempt to let him know what was happening, but it was only confirmed after the fact. Later, my father recalled his fury after learning about what was unfolding. He had tried in vain to call the hospital and organise my release, but he was on the other side of Australia, and he was powerless. The bitter divorce was right at its peak during that time, and arguments had started regarding child support, property settlements, and financial assistance.

Dad had gone to ground to get away from the unrelenting drama. This proved to be the perfect situation to draw him out again and have him forced into communication with a person he was determined to avoid due to the pain she had caused by asking him to leave the family home.

I knew Dad couldn't afford to fly home and save me, but I desperately needed someone in my corner, and I was once again left feeling like a pawn in the middle and wholly abandoned. Once again, who knows what the truth behind the situation was? My father always claimed one thing, and my mother, back then, always claimed another. Each insisted a different story was the truth. I was too young and too lonely to care. I was angry at them both. *Was I ever going to matter enough to anyone? Was I that terrible that even at the age of fourteen, I was written off as a hopeless case?*

Jen came to visit during those days, and I begged her to help get me out. I still remember the tears rolling down her face as the doors locked me back in on one side and her the other. She wasn't able to legally intervene either and was as powerless as me. It was a very hazy time in my life that I have learnt to block out over the years, but I do know it was another day or two before I was released. With the doctor's approval, I was suddenly allowed to stop taking the concoction of drugs I had spent previous months swallowing.

I turned up at school the following week as though nothing had happened, with a face full of perfect makeup hiding my pain and a jumper hiding the scratches on my wrists. For the first time in a long time, as broken as I felt, I also felt seen, just slightly. Enough for them to know that something wasn't right with this cycle of therapists, medication, and lifestyle that had been thrust upon me. Maybe I wasn't the messed-up person that people around me had tried to convince me I was. Perhaps it was the circle around me, the family that I had been born into, that needed to change. Sometimes those closest to you don't always do what is in your best interests. It was a good lesson to learn early on.

The rumour mill has a way of working fast, certainly when a kitchen filled with other school parents saw my downfall. I watched on as the attention and empathy flowed to my 'poor mother' who had such a tearaway and hard-to-control daughter, when all they saw was the smoke and mirrors and not the whole story that occurred behind closed doors. Even my ex-boyfriend Luke had been approached and encouraged to try to help me as I was not in a good place. At that stage, I was barely acknowledging my own existence, let alone anyone else's.

Being released with a clean bill of mental health and no reason for specialised care or medication was exactly what I needed to hear; I knew I wasn't crazy or suicidal. Any faith I had in feeling safe in the home environment with my mother was gone. The damage done to my trust was never able to be salvaged. I felt like I now had to keep this secret that I had been placed in a psych ward for fear that people would never see me the same way again. It was another scar to bear in my increasing necessity to hide who I was. Social services, arranged on behalf of the hospital, stepped in at this point and home appointments were conducted regularly, but I didn't stay at home long after that. I was too terrified of being locked up again without any control, so I packed my school bag with as many clothes as I could fit in there and left.

I spent a few months sharing a bunk bed with a friend from high school whose mother understood the circumstances and tried to help me regain my footing. It allowed me to complete Year 10 at school, which I did without issue. I also thrived without being medicated or having constant therapist appointments, and any anxiety vanished the moment I changed my living arrangements. However, it didn't stop the niggling feeling that I didn't belong anywhere.

The humiliation of having my belongings being carried around in a bag and nowhere that I could call home was too great, and I would often stay with friends of friends who I barely knew so that I could avoid losing face in front of those who knew me. I wasn't able to move in with Joel, as his house rules forbade it, which was understandable. People were worried that, as I was underage, my mother could make a formal legal complaint about me living with an older boyfriend. I refused an offer to move in with Jen's family as I didn't want to burden anyone or let them down any further. I was pushing people away as much as I could so that no-one saw what my life had become.

The new year marked the beginning of 1999 and saw me in a very different circumstance to the year prior. A phone call to Danny made us realise just how far apart our lives were as we spoke about the lost family holidays we had shared only twelve months earlier.

Joel had left school midway through the year to undertake an apprenticeship. He was committed to staying in our hometown for another four years to complete his opportunity to pursue a prosperous career. I, however, didn't think I would be able to last that long in my small hometown anymore.

Joel's mother had gone away overseas for six weeks, and although she had told us both that I was not allowed to stay there, Joel and I relished the fact we could be together, and we spent the time playing house and having a whole lot of fun with our friends. As it grew closer to the time I had to leave, my fear set in. I didn't have anywhere else to turn. I remember going to the real estate office in the main street of Caloundra and looking at units with Joel and his best friend Jax.

The thought was that if they rented out a unit, I could stay and set up a home for myself. In reality, it was never going to happen. I was always asking too much. Joel was young and had a loving, stable home environment, and I was not really the love of his life I had imagined myself to be. I started to pick up signs, and the fear of being rejected again was too much for me to take. Joel said that he wasn't able to move out with me, that we were too young (he was right) and with that one choice, he left me in a position without any real options.

I had no idea how to handle my emotions appropriately, and I learnt very early on how to close down if I thought I was going to be hurt. I believed that our relationship was too young to survive what I was going through, so I saved myself from the shame of becoming a burden and from being hurt first, and I walked away. My father had already left, my relationship with my mother had dissolved, and I had nothing left. Although Joel had been my one constant source of support and love throughout the past year, the pressure of my whole situation was just too much for me, and we broke up in a flurry of tears and devastation. I saw his refusal to help me as a betrayal, as you do when you are young and your emotions are heightened. I was unable to see past the pain of not being good enough for yet another person.

When Jax learnt of my situation, he organised with his stepmother to set me up in their spare room. I thought I had found my knight in shining armour; he wasn't going to sit by and let me stay on the streets. He made me feel seen and valid, as though he recognised the helping hand I needed and insisted on being the one to pull me through. I was hopeful that my saving grace was going to be found within his home and with his family. He protected me, and his stepmother made sure I ate, had a warm bed, somewhere to call home and feel secure. I started to lean on Jax as my confidante, and he helped rebuild my confidence, reassuring me that everything was going to be okay. Slowly, Jax and I became a couple, and instantly this changed the living situation. There was a genuine concern of legal repercussions due to me being fifteen and Jax having just celebrated his eighteenth birthday.

It was explained to me that I could no longer stay there until I was of legal age, and I understood. I tried to hold my head up as I walked out the door, once again with no place to go and my belongings in the school bag on my back.

The first night I had no idea where to go; Jax refused to leave me walking alone and stayed with me as we searched for somewhere safe. It was pouring rain outside, and we were soaked through by the time we came across the local primary school. We climbed over the tall gates and found our way to the bathrooms that had been left unlocked, and with paper towels, I was able to wring out some of my hair at least and change into dry clothes from my bag. After searching for a dry place to hide, we came across some broken-down boxes and placed them on the bottom of the bag racks to cushion the metal base. We huddled under the small space attempting to keep dry as best we could.

We barely slept a wink as the rain loudly came down on the tin classroom roof beside us and splashed up off the concrete ground into the bag racks throughout the night. That was the final straw for me. The word was sweeping around the town about my recent stay in a psychiatric ward, and I felt so claustrophobic that I could barely breathe. Jax kept assuring me that he could look after me, it was all very sweet, and he was doing what he thought was the right thing. But the reality was we were just kids and nothing more than friends who had found comfort in one another. It was certainly not a love story, and we both were well aware of that. The realisation that I had no future in my hometown was becoming more apparent every day.

In the end, a kind couple; Gene and Mandy, who were neighbours in the old cul-de-sac, answered a phone call I made on a payphone late one evening when I realised I was going to be spending yet another night on the streets. *How did it come to this?* I asked myself as I bundled myself into a taxi they ordered. Tears slowly filled my eyes as the car turned into my acquaintances' driveway. They were calm, supportive, and had quickly arranged a spare room for me to call my own by the time I arrived. They took me into their household with open arms and no judgement and let me live there for a month while we tried to look at all my options. Finally, it was decided that I would be packed up and sent to live with my father, who they had contacted in Western Australia, to start over again. I didn't want to go, but more than anything, I wanted to stop being such a burden or inconvenience to everyone around me.

Gene and Mandy contacted my mother in a bid for her and me to try to repair our relationship, but there was nothing left to salvage. When I asked her for my suitcase to pack the little I was allowed to take, I can remember being told something along the lines of, 'You can take your belongings in a rubbish bag as far as I am concerned.' That was one of the last things she said before I left. Thankfully, Mandy organised some striped bags from the discount shop and helped me pack everything I needed.

Jax and I said our goodbyes, and although we promised to stay in touch, I knew that I would never see him again. Joel and I, on the other hand, spent the night before my flight together. We were absolutely devastated at the realisation of what was happening, and any chance of us reconciling and following through with our previous dreams were fading fast. We had never lost contact over the few weeks that I had to stay with Jax, and the pain of what was happening was petrifying to us. We consoled each other as best we could with the time we had left and sobbed as we parted ways for the last time.

The morning of my flight, Gene drove me to the airport and, with tears streaming down my face but knowing I had no options left, I left behind everything I had ever known and boarded a flight that took me to the other side of Australia.

I felt I was living up to this constant sinking feeling that had consumed me since childhood. I believed I was going to be unimportant, entirely unworthy and unlovable, and that I would amount to nothing and be a humiliation to myself for failing such a simple task as living a life that had meaning. With a torn striped bag that held all my possessions and unknowingly pregnant, fifteen-year-old me stepped onto the flight with no idea of what was about to come next.

CHAPTER 2

YOUNG, DUMB, AND BROKE

'Out of the frying pan and into the fire' would probably sum up the next year or two of my life perfectly. The moment my feet hit the tarmac of Perth airport, I knew I was going to turn everything around; I had a chance to start fresh, and I was going to make it work. I had dreams and big plans. I wanted security and a place to call home, with fluffy plush carpet, a soft bed, a fridge filled with food, and a quiet life that no-one could take away from me. I was determined I was going to do what it took it to get there.

I was surprised when I came off the plane and standing beside my father was his new girlfriend. The look on her face said everything I needed to know about how she felt about my arrival. It wasn't long before she became rather vocal about the fact that having children had been an inconvenience she had never wanted in her life, so she made sure to set the tone for my new life quite quickly.

My dream of completing high school had gone out the window instantly as realism took over, and I was asked to scour the job section of the newspaper the very afternoon I arrived. The devastation started to kick in as I mourned for not only the life I left behind but also the future chance I thought I had at rebuilding my new life. I wanted to finish school, meet friends my age, try to reconstruct what had been lost. Instead, I was shown to an empty room with a second-hand ensemble bed on the floor. As I put my bag of meagre possessions down and sat on the bed looking at the emptiness of the room around me, the overwhelming feeling of loneliness swept through me as I took it all in.

Settling into a new life with my father, who was struggling to find his own feet after such a shocking family breakdown, was always going to be hard. I was filled with a mix of unbridled frustration and teenage resentment at life in general at this time, and it was at that moment the veil children see their parents through had slipped. I didn't want to see the human side behind it; I just wanted everything to be okay. I was wracked with guilt at seeming like a burden to everyone, no matter where I turned.

Instead of going back to complete school, Dad informed me that I would be joining the workforce, and I secured a job interview for the very next day. I was hired on the spot for a new food franchise that was opening in a large shopping centre the following week.

So began my not-so-glamorous foray into the workforce. It was nothing like the spectacular career I had planned in my mind, but I tried my best to be positive and was ready to start moving forward and rebuild some stability for myself.

During the week after arriving and before I started my job, I realised something was missing. In a panicked state, I found a local doctor's office, and after blood tests were taken, I sat shell shocked as I was given the follow-up news that I was indeed pregnant. My past had not been left behind so easily, and in secret late-night phone calls back and forth to my hometown, I sobbed desperately. I knew what I would have to do next. I made the devastating decision that I wouldn't have the ongoing support or ability to raise a child, and the heartbreaking choice was made to have a termination.

With the support of my father, who had to sign for the procedure due to me being underage, the last devastating outcome from my time back home came full circle, and I cried myself to sleep for countless nights for my loss. I was broken in every possible way, and from the day I left the clinic, I waited in vain for another phone call to come from Joel but to no avail. It would be almost two decades until I knew the reason why. In the meantime I tried everything I could to forget what had happened in the past twelve months and pretended I was totally fine as I moved on as best I could. I felt like a genuinely despicable human that now had become as worthless and low as people had expected me to become.

I chose to throw my focus into my new work lifestyle, and I relished the independence it brought me. The job was menial and repetitive but also immensely satisfying. I was the youngest member in a team of experienced and, in some cases, much older colleagues, which was a thrilling experience as they all appeared so mature and had the self-reliant security I craved so badly. As I had expected from the outset, the setup of my new home situation was not without issues. We found it hard to find common ground to connect on. With both my father and I trying to find ourselves, it proved too challenging for two emotionally distant people to find a way to support each other through our shared pain. The situation was compounded by my loneliness and feeling disconnected being away from the hometown I'd left—the continued contemplation of what could have been kept me feeling detached and remorseful.

I was fifteen when I went to my first staff party that was put on by the older team members to celebrate a successful first few months in the shop. I went to this house party aware I was considerably younger than most but wanting so badly to fit in with everyone. I sat among everyone on the lounge room floor, drinking vodkas, listening to music, and soaking up as much of my new environment as possible until late into the evening. If I had just taken a taxi home at this point, the entire trajectory of my next few years would have been very different. But hindsight is a beautiful thing, and I had not yet honed my skills of reading people. I had, however, honed my vodka-drinking talents, and at an early hour of the morning dismissed myself from the action and settled into the spare room to sleep it off.

Within minutes, there was a knock at the door from another employee I had become friends with. I'll refer to him as Nick. He was fast approaching his twenty-sixth birthday and seemed both worldly and weary at the same time.

Nick appeared harmless enough and took pity on me. He was compassionate and understood my aspirations for my new life and the pain in leaving behind my old one. That night our friendship became something more serious, and we slept together. I was so lonely and in need of a friend that I was not able to see just how wrong this situation was. Everyone else at the party could, and this instantly rang alarm bells with quite a few other employees, who alerted our boss and owner of the business.

This older and fatherly gentleman took me aside the next week and expressed his concerns that this possibly wasn't the right choice for me. As we sat across from each other at a café near work, he skirted around the issue as delicately as he could.

'I have known Nick for many years, and it has been a favour to his family that I have employed him at my business,' he explained.

I found this choice of words interesting; it was as if he wanted me to realise it wasn't his choice to have him working in his shop.

'I just really need you to be a little careful with your choices. I know you have just moved here and are probably trying to make friends and settle in, and I can see that you are talking a lot together. But I just want you to be aware that maybe he isn't the best person for someone your age.'

I smiled at him and thanked him for his concern, but ultimately I brushed his worries away. I had seen no alarming red flags and thought that maybe, like myself, Nick was just a little misunderstood or had a reputation that belonged in his past.

'We are just friends,' I tried to reassure him, slightly bending the truth as I instinctively knew how wrong the significant age gap appeared. 'I really appreciate your concern, but I am okay, and I can look after myself, and really, it is just nice to talk to someone.' I thanked him for looking out for me.

I knew Nick enjoyed smoking weed; he was also quite open with his other past battles with heavier drugs and some unfavourable behaviour. While I didn't have any experience with most of the stories he spoke about, his company was a nice change after those first few sad, lonely weeks in a new state. At last, I had a companion and someone to talk to and smile with.

When the fact that I was associating with a male considerably older than myself reached back to my father, it didn't go down very well. Nick had visited my house one day before work, and my father instantly saw red. The sight of a man in his mid-twenties who, along with his beaten-up old car, had a permanent smell of marijuana, clearly made Dad size up his bloodshot eyes and intentions in a heartbeat. That sort of behaviour wasn't going to be tolerated by my father.

When I returned from work that evening, Dad let fly: 'Under no circumstances is that person to be anywhere near you or allowed to visit this house ever again.'

The words 'paedophile', 'grooming', and 'drug addict' were thrown around, and I quickly jumped to defend my only friend and refused to even consider that any of these descriptions of Nick were true.

'He is not a drug addict; he struggles with his emotions, and this helps keep him calm.' I tried in vain to make poor excuses, once again, for someone else's poor choices.

'I can't stop being friends with him. I won't have anyone to hang out with, and he drives me to see the other work colleagues, and we catch up to play pool and have dinner together. If I can't see him then I won't be able to fit in here, and I'll be alone again,' I yelled back, resisting his rules.

But Dad didn't back down and told me that he knew trouble when he saw it and Nick was bad news. The rules in his house where to be followed or I could find somewhere else to live. *Here we go again,*

I thought to myself. *No-one trusts my judgement; they all think I'm not able to handle myself.* I was stuck in that strange, lonely state because he had moved there and I wasn't even allowed to have a social life. I couldn't go back to school; I couldn't even choose my friends. I was over this feeling of utter lack of control.

I know my dad thought that if he made such a threat to stop me seeing my new 'friend' or find somewhere else to call home, I would wake up and realise the seriousness of the situation. As a mother now, this makes perfect sense, and Lord help those if this situation ever happened to my children. But at that time, all I felt was that it was just another person willing to quickly get rid of the burden that I felt I had become. Instead of taking Dad's warning on board, I chose Nick. After being given the ultimatum the night prior, I waited until my father had left for work the very next morning, and then Nick arrived in his battered old car and helped me put my bag in the back and I left without even a note.

I can't even imagine what my poor father felt returning home that night and realising what I had done. It is funny what haunts you as you grow older; there are a few moments relating to my dad that hurt my heart—moments like this, I wish I could take back. I felt like the victim at the time, and I really wasn't, but due to the choice I had just made, I was about to become one very shortly, and it was all of my creation.

With a full-time job, I was financially okay to look after myself. But as a fifteen-year-old, I was still underage and therefore unable to sign for a lease or book a hotel room without an adult present. That was easily solved by Nick, who stepped in and said he would help in any way. I must admit I was slightly apprehensive but felt determined to make it all work. Nick had decided he would move out of his parents' house when I left my dad's, and we would move in together. When I went with him to collect his bag of belongings from his parents' lavish home, I was a little surprised that nobody seemed to be concerned that a twenty-six-year-old was moving out into a derelict hotel with a fifteen-year-old girl. In fact, the subject was never raised at all.

*

Initially, we stayed at an incredibly seedy pay-by-the-night hotel room next to a highway, where I was too scared to venture outside by myself. I kept the door locked at all times. I didn't have access to a laundry, but I did have a small shower cubicle, and I would scrub my work uniform on the bottom of the brown-tiled shower floor each night. After wringing it out as tightly as I could, I would roll it in the small worn towel to soak up as much water as possible and hang it up, hoping it would be at least partially dry by the time I had to put it on early in the cold winter morning for my first shift at work. Most times, it was still damp, and I layered a couple of singlets underneath it to soak up the excess moisture.

I would wrap myself in the giant black puffy jacket Jax had given me, and I would wait on the side of the highway as the sun came up to catch my bus to work. I was so unsure of how to do even the simplest things that the first time I tried to catch a bus, I wasn't aware I had to wave it down. I just stood there and watched as it drove straight past, leaving me confused standing like an absolute twit scuffing gravel with my sneakers on the side of the road.

I began to learn life skills very quickly after that; little things such as the fact English muffins are eaten toasted. This was a humiliating realisation as I had been eating them untoasted for years and then watched a television show and stared in shock as a random scene showed the characters pop them into the toaster before serving them. Gee, did I truly enjoy those warm English muffins the very next week when I tried them for the first time. I learnt that iron-on hemming tape is a miracle worker and instantly allows cheap work pants to last a little longer, and double-sided tape can hold together the soles of shoes when they start to fall apart. I always added water to shampoo and cleaning products to make them go further, and I found that if I bought men's clothing, like sweaters or shorts, at the second-hand shops, then it was cheaper than searching in the ladies sections. I had one bra, and I used a safety pin to hold the strap together every day. All of the material issues that I struggled with didn't bother me as much as the looks of pity I received. I recall wearing a woollen sweater to work that had long before started to unravel near the cuff. I had tried to fix it by tying off the wool and also wore it with the sleeves neatly folded up so that no-one could see, but one day it had unravelled so far that it had managed to fall from the elbow, exposing a big split. I pretended that it must have just happened and tried to feign confusion as to what I had caught it on that possibly was responsible for the snag that started it.

I could tell, however, that while people politely pretended to believe me, they also could see the bigger picture: the one pair of shoes that were falling apart and worn the next day again, even if they were still damp from the day prior when I hosed the shop's floor down; the lack of packed lunches, or any lunch most days, and the slight giveaways that maybe I didn't have the same creature comforts that other colleagues around me might take for granted. It didn't bother my belief in myself, but it did hurt my feelings that I possibly appeared to be a lesser human being. I really, really tried never to let that emotion sink into my soul.

I worked until I dropped, doing any overtime offered and spending long hours commuting to save enough money to find a more secure living situation. The timing was convenient as we were soon asked to leave the motel after the police were called due to threats made to the owners by Nick. I recall coming home from work and walking across the road from the bus station as a police car sat out the front of the room we had hired, and instantly I knew Nick was to blame. Sure enough, after being questioned by the police about Nick and his actions (which I had no idea about as I wasn't there when it all happened) we were soon packing our belongings in his battered car again and finding a new place to shelter for the night.

I should have seen the signs then. I think I probably did on a subconscious level, but I didn't have many other options, sadly. At such late notice, the only available option was a run-down caravan park in a somewhat shady part of town. I was able to give a two-week advance payment in return for staying in an old yellow caravan from the '70s with a leaky annexe and a thin double bed mattress in the back. It looked just as tired as I felt.

It would be a weekly rental, as permanent as I needed, and it came with a small gas stovetop, a mini-fridge, and a fold-out table I could use as a kitchen bench. There was a communal grey brick toiletry block with a laundry attached, which certainly made the washing more manageable, but using the shower block late at night after a long shift was quite scary.

The block was open to everyone, and I remember how vulnerable I felt running down the dark path to this poorly-lit block to wash away the day, knowing that a flimsy metal latch on the wooden shower door was the only security I had. I slept with a torch under my pillow and carried it with me in my plastic grocery bag each time I left to visit the laundry or bathroom. It was my only form of protection, but I was becoming more aware and street smart as time went on.

It wasn't situated in the most reputable area of town, but it was all I could afford, and it really opened my eyes to how some other people lived; either by choice or by circumstance. I kept to myself as much as I could, still intimidated by my surroundings, and had decided early on that I was going to keep my head down, work hard, and stay under the radar. I had started to reach out to friends from back home, saving my spare coins and walking to the top of the street to use the payphone. I also wanted to get back in touch with a couple of remaining friends that I had back home on the Sunshine Coast, such as my ex-boyfriend Luke and my friends from primary school, Sam and Amy.

I felt a little more optimistic at this stage and decided I was going to finish high school. There was a school that took enrolments from slightly older kids, who I guess had dropped out earlier like me. It was called Cyril Jackson Senior Campus, and it would allow me to complete my high school certificate. I realised that if I walked half an hour to the train station from the caravan park, took the train to the end of the line, switched tracks, and went for another thirty minutes in a different direction I could make it to school in about two hours. So, I left the safety of my job and became a full-time student. Off I set every day, learning my way around the city as I went. For most of the journey, I'd keep my eyes down and on whatever book I was devouring at the time.

I would rarely be home by 5 pm, and it was bitterly cold during the Perth winters, but I was filled with hope. I was moving in the right direction. I was going to make something of myself, and I was going to do it against all the odds, and the odds *were* stacked. To do my schooling, I had to stop working and relied on government payments to assist in buying food and paying for school fees. I often went hungry, and my weight whittled down to 46 kg on the scales, which saw me be able to step through a plastic coat hanger and pull it over my 167 cm tall frame without an issue. I can remember thinking to myself as I stepped off the train one morning, *I could disappear right now and not a soul in the world would even know.* It was a truly horrible feeling. Not a single family member knew where I was, what I was doing or would be aware if something happened to me. I was truly someone who seemed to become invisible.

I knew how other students at school must have seen me and the assumptions they must have made. I heard the sniggers behind my back when they saw the worn out joggers I still wore from the first day of Grade 8. I had taken to cutting my hair with nail scissors in the toilet block of the caravan park. When I ran out of shampoo, I realised that by rinsing my hair underwater, then applying hair mousse throughout and rinsing it again, it made my locks silky smooth and smelling clean. I bought everything from op shops and still caught the bus on the weekends to the library, where I would sit in a giant bean bag in the corner and read for hours. I would go to the government-supported food shops that sold almost-out-of-date food supplies and stocked up as best I could on the non-perishables, but the money was scarce as Nick seemed to be in and out of work continually.

I remember I used to clean out tins and wrap them in magazine cut-outs and fill them with fresh freesias that grew in the paddock beside the caravan park. I tried my best to attempt to make our space more homely and fill my surroundings with some colour. I managed to make some friends my age at school, and a few asked me over to their house to hang out after class. I didn't even know how to respond most times; I knew Nick was waiting for me at home, and he would start lecturing me on how I was wasting my time at school if I dared to mention anyone else's name. Diary entries that I still have from that time showed how scared I was of his reactions. He would always accuse me of cheating on him, and arguments would flare up if I tried to step out of the depressing world I had been sucked into. It just got easier to withdraw and live a lonely existence than it was to explain that I lived in a caravan with someone over a decade older than me.

It was awkward. Still, I persevered and took up sports and a dance class among my studies. I would come home each night and practise the dance steps in the canopy of the caravan, humming the tune over and over and wishing that I had a radio to listen to music.

After a few months, I realised that the dream I had of finishing school was once again going to have to be put on hold; I needed to get back to work to get out of the caravan park and into the safety of a small house. I wasn't able to save enough money studying to change my future, and I certainly hadn't stopped dreaming of being in charge of my destiny. So I made the executive decision, and I cancelled my enrolment at school and wrote out a resume on the school computers the day before I left.

I walked into the local shopping centre, and I handed out my resume to every shop I came across. Within forty-eight hours, I was employed by Woolworths.

Working there was fantastic for me; they hired me instantly, with no judgement about the young girl standing in front of them clearly in need of a good meal and some proper-fitting clothes. They had no idea about where I was living or my circumstances. When they asked me to get my parents to help me complete my application forms, I just agreed convincingly and brought them back the next day with my signatures in their place without anyone being any the wiser.

For the first time in a long time, I was working alongside kids my age. I had just turned sixteen, and it was nice to share the more relaxed banter between colleagues. I was able to work all holidays, weekdays, and any overtime that no-one else wanted to do, which meant that within weeks I had saved enough money to put a bond down on a small old house with a big open fireplace. As I applied at the real estate, I was told that I couldn't be on the rental agreement as I was under eighteen years old and the house would have to be placed in Nick's name alone. I was starting to feel a little trapped; I was working hard, but still, all my choices and options were at the mercy of someone else. I had hoped that if I could separate myself and get my own place, which I could now afford, then I really would be free to start creating a life without restrictions. Sadly, this was not going to be the case, and without his signature, I would remain stuck in the leaky caravan park until I was eighteen. So I went with the devil I knew and allowed him to sign the rental lease with my money and bond.

Cracks had started to show by now, and associating with groups of thirty-year-olds who seemed to have lost their ambition decades ago and had a penchant for smoking excessive amounts of weed (amongst other things) had made me very uneasy. Still, the caravan park was in a pretty rough end of town, and these were the years the Claremont serial killer was making young girls disappear from the streets of Perth. I was willing to put up with almost anything to have the security of my own home and a front door that I could lock.

The paperwork was signed, and although I was to now be accompanied by Nick in my new house as his name was on the lease, I tried to push aside my fears of his character flaws and moved into my first home. I filled our tiny home with a second-hand fridge, washing machine, and a new bed bought with money I had saved. I had no drawers to put my clothes in, so they sat in neatly folded piles on top of the rattan-type rug that was there when I moved in. I used a packing box as a makeshift bedside table, which I hid underneath a colourful sundress. I didn't have much, but I was thrilled that I finally had somewhere to build a foundation.

The red flags from Nick were now quite noticeable. If I would wear something he didn't like, or he saw me speaking to someone at work, even a customer, I would be accused of trying to get other men's attention. He would become unrelenting in his conviction, and after sometimes days of me trying to subdue his fears, it would always end in him explaining how I had acted in a way that made him uncomfortable. He would listen in on the phone calls I made, staring at me intently if I laughed or had animated conversations. It didn't matter what I did; I always seemed to do something wrong in his eyes. I was consistently being the person begging for forgiveness when I had done absolutely nothing wrong in the first place.

I wasn't able to talk to anyone without him right by my side and as things moved along, this possessiveness just intensified. Before long, the only time I was alone was on the odd occasion when he sat in the waiting room at the doctors during my appointments, and that wasn't very often.

I started jogging in the mornings before or after work and began to regain my confidence. I had the electricity and telephone put in my name. Although I didn't have any real friends in Western Australia to socialise with, I immersed myself back into my books, spending nights poring over dog-eared pages filled with tales of spies from WWII that I had bought from the second-hand shop near my house. I discovered then what I still apply now: even on the hardest of days, a hot shower, clean pyjamas, a cup of tea, and vegemite on toast will make you feel a little better.

I am not sure what made me wake up one morning with a thought in my head, call it woman's intuition, but although I was on the contraceptive pill and my period wasn't late, I thought something felt different. Sure enough, for the second time in my life, two little blue lines showed I was most certainly pregnant again. This time, I was going to make up for everything I couldn't do earlier, and while I was scared, I was also thrilled beyond belief. It felt so right. I knew I was capable of being a loving mother and I would go to the ends of the earth to make sure my child was given everything I had ever dreamed of: a caring home environment, security, and the opportunities they desired.

When the sonographer told me I was having a son, I was elated. I planned everything and read everything I could on parenting and day nursery ideas. I found old wicker cupboards at op shops and spent my spare time painting them yellow and blue. I collected all the nursery items I needed from second-hand shops: a pram, cot, and blankets. I tried my best to create a tiny haven for my son.

I remember reading you need to pre-wash all baby clothes, so I spent an entire afternoon soaking all these tiny bibs, mittens, and grow suits in a tub mixed with a special laundry soaking concentrate. I had set up the clothes horse to hang them all on, and when I returned after the six-hour waiting period, I saw a strange murky colour swirling at the top of the tub. I clearly had read not how to dilute the mixture correctly and sobbed as I pulled out faded and colour-run Bunnykins® bibs and grey cloth nappies. I just had absolutely no-one to turn to for help, so I muddled along on my own.

I didn't have any extra money to replace the damaged clothes, and I had set aside just enough to buy a brand-new outfit for my son when we left the hospital. It was from Pumpkin Patch, which was a big deal and quite expensive at the time. It was a cute navy and white onesie with red trim and an adorable mouse on the pocket. This one went straight into the washing machine, and I admit, to this day, I have never soaked another item of laundry again. It turns out babies don't mind (or know) if their little clothes are second-hand or have weird dye colours from their inexperienced mother's laundry attempts. They will grow up to love you just the same.

I nervously approached my boss at Woolworths when I was starting to show and told them that I knew it wasn't normally acceptable to be seen as a teenage mother. Still, I desperately needed my job and wanted to work until the final few weeks if possible. They didn't even hesitate and supported my choice, providing larger uniforms and allowing me to switch shifts to make doctors' appointments. To this day, I still shop at Woolworths due to the loyalty they showed me. I was so poor back then that a few times I took a roll of toilet paper from the staff room to use at home. I was greatly ashamed and prayed they never noticed. Back then, having a sixteen-year-old pregnant girl at the checkout wasn't how you'd advertise your business. The fact they weren't ashamed of me helped me stay confident. I was reassured by my boss that I had a job to come back to as soon as my baby was born, and I was thrilled with the opportunity they gave me.

As healthy as my baby was, he was making me incredibly ill. I suffered from hyperemesis gravidarum, which brings on severe nausea and vomiting.[1] Trust me to be in the one percent of pregnant women who experience this. Vomiting around the clock led me to be hospitalised a few times for IV fluids. In my final trimester, I developed toxaemia (pre-eclampsia) that posed a significant health risk to myself and bub, and at this stage, I had to leave work and be put on strict bed rest.[2] I couldn't afford any maternity clothes, so I made do with large men's button-down shirts and a pair of blue work overalls from the back of Nick's wardrobe. I relied heavily on the love and support of the Salvation Army, who arrived on my doorstep each week to bring a box of essentials to eat.

My forget-me-not ring from Luke was sold at a pawn shop, and I used the money to buy a nappy bag and a pack of newborn nappies to use when we got home from the hospital. There were no baby showers or celebrations, but I spent my time elated at the thought of being a mother. I was going to live and breathe for this beautiful child, and I knew I would devote my life to being the best mother I could be.

When I was about six months pregnant, I received a phone call from one of Nick's family members. Up until then, I had very little to do with them. They accepted our relationship and seemed to turn a blind eye to the things they wished weren't occurring. What started as a surprise to hear from them soon turned to shock as I discovered the reason for their call: to let me now I had other options available. They stated that as I was so far along in my pregnancy, I could consider adopting my son out after he was born. The phone call was incredibly unexpected, and as I sat in a room filled with the baby items I had begun to collect, I felt intimidated by Nick's parents, who were a well-to-do couple.

I cannot remember how I worded my response, but it was met with a nonchalant reaction, and I said my goodbyes. I soon realised this was how they handled anything: a dismissive swipe, and after that, it no longer affected them in any way. I felt completely alone. Nick had started to tell me he had deep concerns about my parenting ability. He voiced his thoughts that I was superficial and would be too distracted by trying to gain my figure back to give my son the care he would need. I argued that I was entirely competent, but he played on my insecurities and managed to make me feel worthless. It took all my strength to build up a wall against this.

I had experienced enough negativity from people close to me trying to drown my self-worth when I was growing up, and ultimately, Nick's opinions didn't stand a chance. I certainly didn't believe anything he said; I knew that I was going to be a great mother who was selfless and loving, but I could do nothing to convince him of my competence or worthiness.

I'd had my fair share of discrimination by this point, and one particular day, I was chased out of a newsagency by the owner. He yelled at me, swung me around and yanked a magazine that I had tucked under my arm while accusing me loudly of stealing. Then, he looked down, and when he realised it was a free real estate magazine the neighbouring business had given me, he didn't even apologise or seem embarrassed. He just thrust it back at me and stormed back into his shop.

Overall, people just pointed and muttered under their breath. I didn't let it bother me too much, and the kindness being shown by the midwives and the Salvation Army made up for the few moments of cruel taunts from random strangers.

During my regular antenatal appointments, midwives gently expressed concerns about my safety and living arrangements. They had noticed the age gap and the very drug-affected Nick who would show up to the clinics. They even asked him point-blank if he was taking drugs. To my horror, he openly admitted it. I just shrank back further into my seat, embarrassed for myself. I was, at this stage, helpless. Once again, I had no-one to turn to, and the only joy I had in my life was the long-awaited arrival of my beautiful son.

I became a mother on a rainy Wednesday in June and Rhyz came into the world after almost nineteen quite traumatic hours of labour. As I had complications during the delivery and then haemorrhaged after his birth, the nurses decided after I had initially held him for a moment that he would be safer in his crib, as I might accidentally drop him due to my fatigue. I can remember expressing how I desperately wanted to try to breastfeed my son, but they told me I wasn't up to it and to try the following day. They then left me on the table, still covered in the blood-soaked hospital gown and went to have their tea break.

Nick, who had remained drug-free during the labour, also saw this as an opportunity to duck home and have a celebration before making his way back to the hospital later that evening. I just lay there and stared at my gorgeous son on the other side of the room all tucked up in his crib, and I couldn't believe I had become a mother to such a beautiful boy.

I had no family and no friends visit me in hospital, and I refused to let Rhyz out of my sight. Back then, they took newborn babies into the nursery each evening, but I insisted he stay right next to my bed and I could not stop staring at this absolute piece of heaven I had the blessing of calling my own. The three days in the hospital were incredible. I was given meals at each opportunity, my room was heated, and the security doors made me feel safe for the first time in years. I also felt incredibly nervous someone would come along and take my son from me. It was all overshadowed by the fear I had of being so young and my only support being someone who was starting to show their true colours and was certainly not a responsible role model.

I had to play along, I had to make a plan, and I most certainly wanted so much more for my son. I dreaded leaving the hospital and going home to a rundown old house that only featured carpet in the bedroom after a piece was bought to keep in some warmth. The house itself was earmarked for demolition within months, which gives you a clear idea of its condition. There was no money coming in, other than from the government pension, and the house was being frequented by shady older individuals who wanted to partake with Nick in unsavoury activities.

I thought during my pregnancy that I could protect my son, that I was going to be able to turn a blind eye to Nick's activities, or at least control the situation better. But I knew I had no power. I had been told so, if not by the threats and menacing behaviour, then most certainly by the fact that I had experienced being left out in the cold before. I wasn't going to let it happen to my son. When we came home, nothing had changed, and I spent my days singing softly to my son as I cradled him in an old peeling pleather chair that had been found in the kerbside rubbish collection. I had covered it with a crocheted blanket from the op shop. I started to plan how I was going to get us out of our situation.

I remember the humiliation of calling my nana and pop in New Zealand with utter excitement to let them know that my son was born. They admitted they had only just told their neighbours of my 'situation'. At that moment, I realised just how ashamed of me my family was. I told them that I had given my son the same middle name as my pop and I recall my nana on the phone questioning if I really wanted to do that. No-one ever made the trip to see us or meet my baby boy. I knew that I was alone, just him and me against the world, and no-one was coming to save me. I was going to have to do it myself.

When Rhyz was only two weeks old, the front door was broken off its hinges in one of Nick's fits of rage, which left me scrambling to the safety of one of Nick's relatives. Their place, however, was no refuge. Upon walking through the door, what I was told was essentially 'you made your bed, now lie in it'.

Well, I thought to myself quietly, *that is not how I see this; if you make your bed and you don't like it, get the fuck up and move on. You are not stuck.* So, in a last desperate attempt to salvage our future, I used every last cent I had in the bank account and booked a flight back to the Sunshine Coast, the place I had said I would never return to again until I had made something of myself.

I came back with only one thought in mind, and that was my son's future. I would endure any humiliation my reappearance would trigger. He was four weeks old when we boarded the plane and Nick only let me leave with Rhyz if I had a return ticket. It was made very clear I was never allowed to take his child away from him. I had managed to convince him I wanted to have my son meet my mother. We'd had a non-existent relationship since I left, but I was desperate to escape and thought this excuse to be the most plausible. It was clear from the moment I walked off the plane that it had been a huge mistake. Nothing had changed; the tension was palpable, and I felt terribly uncomfortable. I felt like I was a massive inconvenience, and I certainly didn't belong there. Now there was a man who shared her home too, and it felt like I was intruding. It was not the welcome I had expected. I am not sure why I had ever thought it would be different. I guess I'd hoped having my son would maybe give my mother and I a relationship base that we'd never had before, or at least have the common understanding of motherhood to bond over. Instead, it made it harder for me to comprehend her role and her attitude towards me—her daughter. I just felt lower and more useless each passing moment I was there. Demeaning comments and ridicule were passed in my direction by those surrounding us, and I knew then that my son would never know a grandmother—the type you see in the movies running with arms open for hugs and fresh cookies in the kitchen ready to share. It was not going to work. Luke, however, was at my doorstep within moments of my arrival, and for the time I was there, he only left my side to go to work.

The rest of my school friends were in their final year at high school, and a few old friends from the past came by to visit and see my little bundle of joy. Sam, Kirsten, and another friend Matt, who all went to primary and high school with me, happily spent time with my son and offered words of encouragement to me in those early days. It meant so much to me as I felt incredibly vulnerable. Other girls from my grade called me a slut when I was in earshot, and I died inside thinking this is what I brought my son home to.

Rhyz was a sweet baby who slept well and smiled broadly; he was an absolute dream come true. I knew that coming back to my hometown had been a bad idea; everyone I knew still lived at home and was going about an entirely different life to me. Their focus was not like mine anymore. I was going around in circles and losing ground quickly. As I stood in the hometown that was surrounded by the rubble of my parents' failed marriage, it just reiterated how much I didn't want my child to grow up without a father present. But more than anything, I didn't want my son growing up where my reputation preceded his, and he was 'that child' of 'that troubled teenager'. I needed to think fast and act even faster as I wanted stability for Rhyz.

Luke gallantly stepped up and offered to take on the role of father and all the responsibilities that came with it, but I refused. I was still carrying the inner feeling of being a burden to everyone, and he had a fantastic apprenticeship and future opportunities. I was sure Luke would grow to resent me if I took away his youth as well; he was only seventeen himself. He came around one afternoon and had organised for a car seat attachment to be fitted into his truck, so Rhyz could easily be part of any future endeavours. It was a sweet thought, but it instantly made me panic. Luke still lived at home, and his apprenticeship meant he worked away a lot.

He couldn't support us, and I didn't want him to take on the stress. More than anything, I didn't want him to have to change all the wonderful things he had going on for a situation I had gotten into myself. It was clear to me just how important Luke's friendship had become to me throughout the last few years. I couldn't risk losing his respect like I had others who walked straight past me in the street as though they had never seen me before.

One morning it struck me: *Maybe I was immature, and surely everyone deserves to grow up knowing their father. Maybe I had been too hasty.* Nick kept calling, promising he would find a home for us and he would get a job. He wanted to change and assured me everything would be okay.

I was continually reminded by Nick that I was young and immature and that I needed to work at a relationship and quite possibly had my life expectations set too high. (For anyone who may ever be told this, it is usually said by people who have set their life expectations too low.) The guilt of taking a child away from his father soon ate away at me and being back home inside the fractured remains of what was once my family made me start to question my ideas. I also knew that without a custody order in place, I wasn't able to stay in Queensland. I was trying my best to bide my time, hoping that I would be allowed to stay away. But the phone calls and reminders that I needed to bring Rhyz back started to make me fearful. I didn't want to risk losing my baby, certainly not when I knew I had no support and Nick's family would make a scene if I tried to run.

So my initial plans of breaking free and setting up a new life back in my hometown started to wane. I didn't want to be like my mother. I had no bigger fear in the world than to make my son feel the way I did growing up. So, with no role model or person to guide me and talk me through my options, I boarded a plane back to Perth and sealed my fate.

In the couple of weeks that I was away, Nick had managed to be kicked out of the house. He was also taken to court over stolen goods. The bed that I had left behind had somehow been burnt in a field, according to those who knew him.

Nick managed to be saved again by his family. They had organised a small house on their friend's property to move into when I returned. A bed had been hastily made with some scrap lengths of wood, and I tried to keep my head up as I knew this was now a future I had chosen. I needed to make the best of it for the sake of our son. I was committed now; I had to make this work. I was going to try harder and be more understanding and try to make the family I wanted so badly for my son.

I wasn't able to drive as I had never had a chance to learn, let alone have a car to learn in, so I was somewhat at the mercy of Nick, who accompanied me everywhere now. The house we had moved into was in a rural setting on the outskirts of town with no close access to buses or shopping centres. The nearest phone box was a forty-five-minute walk away, next to a small grocer. All in all, it was quite secluded. There was a property at the top of the hill just above us, and they kept a small horse in the large paddock, which sat in front of our small stilt home. This horse brought great joy to Rhyz, who loved to spend time on his swing on the veranda watching the horse run around.

I started back at work a few days a week, and I put Rhyz into a local daycare so we could once again start moving forward. I was driven to work and collected daily by Nick; there was no breathing room at all. I was at the whim of the person who terrified me. When marriage was discussed and two second-hand wedding bands bought from a local pawn shop, I felt I had no further excuses.

Nick drove me to an elderly celebrant's house of an evening to sign the paperwork of our impending marriage when I was still seventeen years old. I hid my eyes from the concerned look that was being given as this kindly man stared at my tiny teenage frame holding my baby and Nick's towering six-foot stature. Nick took over choosing every vow, how the proceedings on the day would run, and even the song I would now walk down the aisle to, as he appointed his sister my bridesmaid.

Knowing that I had truly started down a path I could not escape from, I began to long for some form of protection. I told Nick I wanted to reconnect with my father. He didn't hesitate when he commented gloatingly, 'I bet he will be very surprised to see we have a child together now.' I knew that if I played on his ego, I might be allowed to have someone in my life who could be a safety net. I went back to the old house, but Dad had moved on. Thankfully, the new occupants had his address, and I was able to track him down. With Nick in charge all the way, we drove up my dad's driveway, and I do not know how my father held it together, but he shook Nick's hand and hugged me tight and then got the surprise of his life when I opened the back door and the bright-eyed Rhyz grinned broadly from the back seat.

He never mentioned a word about my choices and showed nothing but support for my son and me. My eighteenth birthday came two weeks later, and I celebrated with pizza and cake with my son in our little lounge room.

Six days after I turned eighteen, I walked down the aisle and promised for better or for worse with Nick. I had just married a man who was about to celebrate his thirtieth birthday.

The negativity escalated at a rapid pace before the wedding photos were even printed, and what were once threats turned into physical confrontations. With Rhyz under one arm, I was thrown into a kitchen bench so hard that as I lay screaming in pain from the hit, I realised with fear that I couldn't move my legs. They lay in front of me but stubbornly would not cooperate with my mind's commands to lift me off the floor. I was left there, unable to feel my lower body, while being tormented from the other side of the room until I slowly began to regain feeling and managed to stumble to my feet and limped with fear into the bathroom to hide.

Nick left the house not long after, knowing I was unable to leave anyway, and using his mobile phone (I didn't have one) that had almost miraculosly been left behind upon his exit, I called my father for help straight away. Dad had changed a lot in the time he stepped away from the family home, and his past substance issues were no longer as hidden as they once were. This day, for whatever reasons, he was unable to drive and instead told me to call a taxi, and he would pay for it at his end when we arrived. Little Rhyz and I packed a day bag and set out to my father's house. When I got there, I thought, *Maybe I have overreacted,* and I started to panic at what would happen if I stayed away too long. I made sure that I was back in time to organise dinner, and Nick was none the wiser that I had left at all when he returned later that evening. I don't know what I wanted, but I knew that I needed saving, I just didn't trust anyone that was around to be there in the right way. Nick and my father both partook in activities that weren't exactly above board, and Nick started to threaten that if I ever left, he would make sure my father paid the price for my disloyalty also. I was stuck.

The couple from the house on the hill above ours called in one evening to check that everyone in the house was safe after hearing cries and shouting. Seeing the obvious holes that had been put in walls and doors, they expressed sincere worry, but it was quickly explained away, even if it was unconvincing. I had family violence pamphlets left in the letterbox by those concerned neighbours.

The police and ambulance had been called when I had to jump from our car when it slowed to turn a corner on the main highway after Nick had sideswiped cars and veered into other lanes. I managed to move fast enough that I flung open the back door and grabbed Rhyz from his car seat. We were rescued by another car that had stopped to help when he saw Nick's irrational behaviour in the driver's seat. After this sort of behaviour, I would find my way home and sit there awaiting the fury that would surely come through the front door soon after. I could no longer do anything right; I just copped the brunt of it all. I started to develop pain in my chest, and after repeated requests, I was taken to the doctor, who sent me to the hospital for tests. They couldn't find anything wrong, but the pain continued. Then one evening there was an accident, and with Rhyz in my arms. I found myself falling into the fireplace; I reached my other arm out and stopped myself by holding on to the burning hot flue.

The skin on my hand instantly burnt, and the pain was excruciating. I was taken directly into the emergency room. Nick kept a close eye on me as the doctors and nurses asked questions about what had happened. I was treated, given pain relief, and my throbbing hand was wrapped in a massive bandage. I was sent home and advised to follow up with the local doctor. Now, this local doctor was also the person Nick had seen for years about all sorts of health issues he had:

mental illness, drug abuse, physical ailments, etc. and this gentleman must have been waiting for an opportunity to present itself.

When I was taken to him for a follow-up appointment relating to my hand, he asked Nick to take baby Rhyz into the waiting room so he could do a few more stress tests on my heart. He told Nick he had results back from the hospital and wanted to check a few more things.

I was surprised and thought I had the all-clear, but I handed Rhyz over and thought no more of it. The moment the doors closed, however, the doctor started to ask me questions regarding our relationship, and in no uncertain terms, he expressed I needed to leave before it was too late. He said I was never to tell Nick we had spoken, and whatever I had to do, do it fast. I was shocked; I wasn't aware anybody noticed, let alone cared enough to say anything. But he did, and I was grateful that for the first time in a long time, someone had said it wasn't okay to stay in that situation.

I was now degraded to sleeping on the lounge room floor with a blanket and a pillow, ('like the dog I was') although this did have the upside of keeping as much distance between Nick and myself as possible, and I knew that the time had come to get out. I had been hiding a small portion of my wages each week behind photos in an old album among my collection of books. One week when I went to add another note, I realised everything was gone. It was no use confronting him; it would have only made for another fight. I had no phone, no car, and even if I tried to take his car to escape, I didn't know how to drive. I kept waiting for the right opportunity to present itself. I was never going to leave without my son, and Nick had clearly become aware of my intentions. He had stopped work, so he was at home around the clock, making sure I was never left alone.

With Nick's erratic behaviour escalating, I knew I had to act soon. One evening, I decided I was going to leave the next morning. My fear was so real that I felt if I stayed any longer, I would be killed.

I woke at sunrise and crept into Rhyz's room. I packed a few essentials into his nappy bag, added a couple of sets of his clothes, some baby food and bottles, and hid it in the bottom of the pantry as I set about getting everything else ready. I had left the pram on the front veranda the night before after using the excuse of washing it during the day and leaving it open and out overnight to dry. I suddenly heard an alarm go off in Nick's room and listened as he woke up and started down the hallway. I slid quickly back under the blanket on the floor, facing the other way and praying he thought I was asleep and hadn't suspected my intentions. *Why on earth was his alarm set? He doesn't have a job.* I lay there, listening intently, as Nick made his way into the nursery, picked up a still sleeping Rhyz and took him back into his bed with him. I heard the rustling of the duvet as he settled back to bed with our son tucked securely by his side.

My mind was racing, I don't know what I had done to make him realise what I was about to do, but he had clearly been one step ahead of me, and now I was stuck. *What excuse could I possibly use to extract Rhyz out of his arms so that we could escape?* Worse still, I needed Nick to be asleep when I tried to leave. The house was halfway up a hill; it was at least a kilometre to the letterbox at the end of the driveway. From there, I could only use one main open road to get to the phone box I needed to reach, which was usually around a forty-five-minute walk away. I couldn't let him be awake or even be woken by my leaving. I needed a good head start, and I knew I only had one chance at it.

The answer came almost so easily I didn't expect it. When Rhyz stirred awake in the bedroom, I quickly dashed in to pick him up, mumbling about having a bottle all ready for him and brought him back to the lounge room for his breakfast, hoping that Nick wasn't woken fully by this and would go back to sleep. I fed Rhyz with bated breath as I waited to hear further movement from the bedroom, but there was nothing. This was it; this was my one chance to escape.

CHAPTER 3

UNDER MY THUMB

I quietly pulled on my old, purple school joggers and quickly retrieved the packed nappy bag from the hiding place in the pantry. I must have paced on the spot for a minute, building up courage, before slowly opening the front door and cautiously stuffing the nappy bag in the bottom of the pram on the veranda. I went back to the end of the hallway to make one last check for movement from the bedroom, and then with painfully slow movements, I pulled the door closed behind me.

Within a quick breath, I had Rhyz strapped into his pram and then looked in front of me, realising a fatal flaw in my plan. At the end of the veranda, which finished just bedside the bedroom window, was about ten metres of loose gravel in the driveway. I was bound to make a racket once the pram wheels hit it in the quiet of the morning.

Too late to back out now, I took about six paces to the end the veranda and then ran full speed down the loud driveway with stones flying up behind me.

I hit the asphalt at the end and must have broken land speed records with the pace I was going! By the time we had turned onto the main road headed for the shops, my lungs were burning, but my legs were driven by pure adrenaline. I swerved the pram every time I looked back over my shoulder to check he wasn't following us. Eventually, I gave up on looking for him and stared straight ahead, not slowing for a second. I was shaking like a leaf by the time I made it to the phone box, and I pushed the numbers I had to my father's house, praying he would answer and not judge me for what I was about to say to him.

Thankfully, he was home, and without a hint of judgement, assured me he was on his way. I was still in a public space while I made this call and was instructed by Dad to hide while he drove to me.

'Cross the road to the grocer's and tell them you need to hide. Ask to go in a backroom or, at worst case, a walk-in freezer. I don't want him to see you before I get there,' Dad instructed.

I hung up the phone and sprinted across the road and stayed hidden in the shop until I saw Dad's bronze station wagon pull into the carpark. I was bundled into the back seat of the car, and we took off. Dad turned the car back up the street towards the direction I had just come from; I squealed in panic as he exclaimed he was going in to get the cot for Rhyz and tell Nick we would not be returning. I sat, barely breathing, in the driveway, watching Dad storm up the gravel path to the house and throw open the front door.

Within a few moments, he exited holding the dismantled cot, the mattress—still with sheets attached—and a bag filled with toys. He opened up the back of the station wagon and threw them inside. He left it open, and without saying a word disappeared back inside the house only to emerge with an armful of my clothes. This time, he shut the boot and got back in the driver's seat and reversed at top speed. Not once did Nick emerge from the house.

I was told that Nick was warned, in no uncertain terms, to not move from the bed he was still lying in, or attempt any contact with me at all, and the divorce and custody orders would be organised within the week.

We drove off to the safety of Dad's home, and he set Rhyz and me up in his room for the night while he took the couch by the door to make sure we were safe. I slept soundly for the first time in months. Within twenty-four hours of my escape, I had made all the phone calls to the appropriate agencies to make the separation permanent and organised to have legal custody papers drawn up so Nick could have regular visitation. That was done in August. We had walked down the aisle only weeks earlier in June. The fairytale, and the façade that went with it, was officially over.

The first visitation was nerve-wracking as Nick came to collect Rhyz and me from our new address and we went to a public park. He spent time playing with Rhyz while we had a coffee; it seemed to be going well. He understood it had been an unhealthy environment, and he was incredibly apologetic.

As we pulled into my driveway to drop us home, I felt relieved and surprised by how smoothly it had gone. We planned another playdate for the following weekend. We were making general small talk about our separate plans for the rest of the day. Nick asked what my dad was up to, as his car wasn't there when we arrived. I explained how he had gone out and thought nothing else of it as I unbuckled Rhyz from his seat and we turned to wave Nick off as he slowly reversed down the driveway.

I turned my back to unlock the front door with Rhyz tottering near my feet when I heard the car engine rev hard. The tyres squealed as the car sped back towards us. I couldn't get the keys out to open the front door fast enough, and within a heartbeat he was out of the car and had picked Rhyz up by the back of his denim dungarees with one arm, yelling threats in my direction. I sprinted past him towards his car and reached in through his open door in an attempt to pull the keys out of the ignition, so at the very least he couldn't leave with Rhyz. But his towering frame and his rage overpowered me. While still holding our son with one hand, he managed to hurl me out the way and onto the dirt and gravel driveway with such force that burn marks from my sweater were left on my collarbone from the speed and severity of the action.

Before I could scramble to my feet, he had thrown Rhyz into the front passenger seat and was reversing at high speed back down the driveway. I watched in horror as my one-year-old son was thrown forward onto the floor with the force of the speed. I chased his car as far as I could onto the road, screaming at the top of my lungs for help, but to no avail.

I raced back to the house and managed to open the door with the keys shaking in my hand and called my dad in a complete state of hysteria. While I was still trying to explain what had occurred through blubbering cries, the car once again came swerving into the driveway from the street. The passenger door was opened from the inside. Rhyz was hauled out of the car and roughly put back at the same front door where this drama all began only moments earlier. Nick sped off again, this time leaving both a hysterical toddler and me behind.

I raced inside and locked every door and window, pushing the dining room table against the door just in case he came back. I called Dad again and begged him to come home and that I was calling the police to come and look after us. Dad's words made me freeze: 'Don't call the police! I am a little inebriated and in a taxi with my friends heading out for the night, and the police can't come to my home and see me in this state, or they'll have my home on their radar. I have turned the taxi around, and I will be there soon, it will be okay.'

I locked Rhyz and myself in the bathroom and counted the seconds until he arrived home again. I was being protected and saved by someone who I didn't morally agree with, but I had nowhere else to go.

I decided to go to the police station and make a formal report. Photos were taken of the marks on my neck and the bruises that covered my body—injuries sustained when I was thrown to the ground. I opened up and explained the previous incidents that I had endured and the genuine fear I had that I seriously felt my life was in danger. After going through all the legal hoops, I was granted a temporary domestic violence restraining order against Nick. I had to wait with bated breath for the papers to be served upon him for them to come into effect. In the meantime, while they searched for him, he was under no legal order that protected me from his wrath. I knew he was going to explode when he realised I had gone to the police for help.

I was given the option to pursue legal charges, but I was too scared of any retaliation and lost in the fear that had held me for so long; I didn't know how to stand up for myself. The police maintained communication, and after a couple of days, Nick was located, and they could finally confirm that he had been served the restraining order papers. They then assured me Nick was being relocated immediately, thanks to his family, in an attempt to curb any change of heart I may have had with pressing charges.

Before the sun had set on the following day, Nick was moved to the bottom of Western Australia, and I felt I could start to rebuild my life with some form of a safety barrier. All that protected me was a flimsy piece of paper that I had to carry on my person at all times in case he appeared and broke the conditions that had been set out for him. Still, it was a start at standing up for myself in the smallest way possible and refusing to let my life be filled with constant fear. There was a court date I had to attend to make the domestic restraining order permanent and with no contest or denial from Nick (who was not in attendance and rumoured to be in yet another stint in rehab), I was relieved when the judge didn't hesitate to make the protection order permanent, after hearing the extent of what had occurred in the past few years.

I refuse, however, to ever refer to myself as a victim of domestic violence. Until a couple of years ago, I had kept the fact this had even occurred to me as a very tightly held secret. I never wanted to be defined by a term that is inflicted on me; it means the person who caused the pain and abuse has given you a name to wear forever. I am not a victim; I have risen against it and used the trauma and lessons learnt to build the foundations of the strong and self-empowered woman I am today. I have chosen to look at it as a terrible experience in my life that took up way too much of my soul than it ever should have, and I will not allow it to be part of even a small section of my life anymore.

While there were many more issues in the years to follow, Nick was never a major fixture in my life ever again. There were future court battles, extra police patrols past my home in the following years to make sure Rhyz and I were safe, and plenty of pure, white-cold fear. Nick's photo was placed at schools and daycares with copies of the DVO and child custody paperwork, and I always looked over my shoulder. I still have to enter my home and check every room, cupboard space, and wardrobe before I settle. It has become a habit, and I am unaware of it until someone points it out to me. I still jump at loud noises, and I instinctively crumble to the ground with my hands over my head if anyone jumps out and surprises me. I sleep with every light on except for the bedrooms. I still wake in a cold sweat some nights, although it has started to lessen in the past few years.

Some years followed of intermittent terror where unexplained happenings would occur and leave me petrified; I once was unable to start my car one morning, and when I opened the bonnet, I found a butcher's knife sitting on top of the disconnected battery. I had no-one to protect us, and at some stage, I just felt that I had as much freedom as I was ever going to get. I tried hard to ignore the fear that followed me around.

It is strange, though, as the fear of him has never gone away. No matter how many years pass or how many miles are between us, I don't think it ever will. I know what he is capable of, and even the thought of writing this down took more courage than I ever expected I would need. I never pursued charges on the threats and violence as I was too scared of the repercussions. The domestic violence restraining order was the only record I fought to get, and with the police photos of my injuries and the official statement made, there was no denial from Nick. He accepted it without me having to fight for my protection. I never called the police or other agencies for help as I was so scared of what would happen if it went wrong, and he was able to get access to me when I wasn't protected.

Nick came from a very well-to-do family who had plenty of financial backing to engage all the lawyers in the world and an uncanny ability to turn a blind eye and brush things under the rug for fear of losing face. I came from nothing, with my only support available from government legal aid.

While my son was encouraged to continue his relationship with his father, it was a heartbreaking and scary time during every visit when I had to say goodbye. The legal system explained clearly that there was no violence shown to my son. Therefore, he was still allowed access as often as the courts dictated. Rhyz went there with a toy lamb named 'Lamby' that we had customised to have a small hole in its back.

It was where I would hide emergency phone numbers and money for him if he needed to get help. Sadly, Rhyz had to use this a couple of times. He was even put in the position at the age of five, where he had to run to the grocery store and ask a store attendant to call an ambulance as he couldn't wake his dad.

I didn't have a legal leg to stand on. Nick was entitled to visits regardless of the lack of care he may have given, his violent history with me, or his past criminal history. It came as no surprise their relationship was always marred by dysfunction on Nick's end.

The final straw that made Rhyz choose to break away on his terms was when he finally found the courage to stand up to his father. In a recorded telephone call from the safety of an address unknown to Nick, Rhyz told him he'd had enough of it all: all the drugs, of sleeping in the same rooms he grew his drugs in, of his toys being sold, being taken on drug deals, and having his money stolen to purchase drugs.

As I heard my teenage son becoming louder and more confident on this phone call, my mouth dropped open in horror, as I had never been told the extent of what he had to endure. Rhyz had kept it a secret as he was so embarrassed by Nick's actions; it was such a painful conversation to hear. Nick responded that drugs had been in his life before his son came along, and he would essentially be choosing that over him as Rhyz should not be allowed an opinion on the subject. Nick had the audacity to compare it to a child telling their parent not to have a glass of wine at night. He didn't deny anything; he wasn't even upset their relationship was being severed.

The hurt that conversation caused was the final fracture in a ticking time bomb of a relationship between us all, and it cemented Rhyz's decision. That was the last time Rhyz spoke to him. He took it upon himself to change his name by deed poll the week of his eighteenth birthday to erase any connection to Nick in any way, shape, or form. It was a very healing moment for us all when that happened. He had already chosen to be known by a different surname from the age of ten, but it wasn't able to be done in the courts until he was legally an adult.

That part of our lives never defined me, and it certainly didn't define Rhyz. In fact, it showed him exactly who he never wanted to be, and that there was no trace of any of that family's genetics running through Rhys's veins. I have waited over twenty years now for Nick to come after me, and while I am still terrified, I am not going to be scared into silence any longer.

But back to where we were, with Nick far away and police protection in place, my life blossomed, and Rhyz and I began to create a beautiful life that I had spent years waiting to achieve.

My father had decided to accept a job not long after the restraining order was set in place, and this position would see him work away for long periods at the top of Western Australia. It meant that ours would become a sporadic relationship. Some periods would see us connect and support each other; a tiny family of three. Yet, other times our relationship would be a disjointed confusion about where we would stand with one another.

I owe much to Dad. He may not have always known how to be the perfect father, but he never turned me away, and he allowed me to pick up the pieces of my broken life without ever passing judgement. He allowed me and Rhyz to sleep in his bed while he slept on his couch in those early days before he bought Rhyz and me a bed. He would sometimes be my greatest everything, and at other times, he could be hurtful and discouraging. I always know that he would be there if I needed him, but it was common for us to go months and even years without contact.

It has been over six years without communication now, and he has missed so many pivotal life moments, which he sadly won't ever get back, but somehow that was the way it went for us.

He was still, without a doubt, the best parent I had. No-one is perfect, not even I, not even close, but he tried the very best he could, and that is all you can do as a parent. I will always, always love him deeply, flaws and all. He taught me a lot, and I am grateful for the times he saved me. Without him, I don't know where I would have ended up.

It isn't as though he doesn't love me; I know he does. I just think our years of divide and the generations of not knowing how to keep a family together stopped us from having something more substantial. It used to break my heart, but then I realised I was only hurting myself by caring too much about something I cannot change. I wish it were different. Though like a lot of parts relating to my family, it just isn't, and I am strangely, calmly okay with that now. Because of him and the strength he had to change the negative impact his toxic family had on him, I was able to do the same, and the cycle stopped right there.

I would sit in my father's spare room on my blue futon bed that doubled as a lounge chair, and I remember I wrote a list of what I wanted. As I worked my way through crossing off those goals, I could feel my confidence and self-esteem rebuild with each step I accomplished. A year later would see me, at nineteen years old, living in a four-bedroom rental with a huge backyard for Rhyz to run around in, supporting myself entirely in the lovely place I had made into a cosy home for us both.

I had spent my time learning how to cook everything from roast dinners to healthy stir-fries, and was able to stand proud as I independently provided a caring environment for my son. I had finally secured my driver's license and even had a car to call my own. I also had managed to secure a dream job working for a university and combined community library, which filled my heart and intellectual mind with joy.

I also finally managed to complete my high school studies at night externally through TAFE when it clashed with my work shifts and finished it all with flying colours. Rhyz attended the daycare on the campus, and I was allowed to check him out during my break so that we could share lunch at the cafeteria before my next class or shift started. I was proud of myself, and while I may not have graduated in 2000 with the rest of my classmates, I still held my head high that I had persevered and got it done.

It was essential for me to set a good example for my son. I wanted to provide him with the best future possible and, more than anything, demonstrate to him that with hard work comes great reward.

At nineteen, I finally started to be able to relax a little more and made some lovely friends who were studying at the university where I worked. I began to enjoy living the life I had created. I started volunteering at the local museum and was fascinated with archiving and, more specifically, the thought of maybe one day working in the war archives.

I studied history after I put Rhyz to bed at night time, reading every subject ranging from American presidents to the world wars, British intelligence, and everything in between. I fell in love with scouring vintage shops and spent each weekend carting a box of toy dinosaurs to the beach with Rhyz to soak up the sun and find the groove in our routine. It was the start of me finding my feet in the world. I had successfully built my foundation, and I would make sure no-one would ever take that away from me again.

I was happily single and a dedicated and focused mother. Homesickness was always there, but I knew I would not return for quite some time as I had a lot of living to do first and I was okay with that. Mobile phones were common now, and I was able to keep up to date with my friends back in Queensland. This contact helped me feel less alone. It is funny, but those people from primary and high school that I kept in touch with every step of the way all played significant roles in my life, even to this day. They were my family, and I am proud that they still are.

I was no longer the broken and scared little girl who had no options and was under the thumb of some else who held all the power. I was self-assured and confident in my own right, and I was just getting started.

I had big goals for us, and I wanted to be able to start saving for a small home that we could call our own. I knew I was going to have to step it up and work twice as hard to make that a reality.

I enrolled in external studies to begin my journey to become a librarian, with the end goal being to work among the war archives. Even if I didn't get that far, a life spent among the books was going to make me incredibly happy.

As I began to juggle the heavier course loads, work shifts, and motherhood, I realised I wasn't going to be able to keep up with it all. Attending university full-time to study the courses I had a passion for wasn't going to be an option for me; I was not going to be able to afford the fees and all my living expenses. I chose to do what I thought was the smartest and best decision for me at the time, and that was to work as hard as I could with the opportunities that came my way. When I had provided my son with the opportunities to follow his dreams, I would still be young enough to chase my own dreams then. I dropped the extra study courses and focused on finding an additional way to secure our future.

I was reading the local paper one afternoon looking for a second job to make up the hours from my part-time library assistant position, and a particular advertisement caught my eye. It had flexible hours, great pay, and it was right in town, not far from my home. I met the requirements they were searching for: young, fit, and confident. I thought it over for a couple of days, then I made the call, and before I knew it, I was walking into Zelda's Strip Club for an interview.

CHAPTER 4

POUR SOME SUGAR ON ME

Zelda's Strip Club in Rockingham was an experience all on its own; it had one heck of a reputation in town and attracted quite a big crowd back in the day. The fact that it was right near a naval base was the pure marketing genius of the owner, who also owned the nightclub next door, which meant patronage was never short and the lines to get in were always long.

Now, I had never set foot in a strip club; at this stage, I don't believe I had ever been to a night club either. I was entirely curious, and the thrill of glamourous costumes covered in sequins, flowing champagne, and random celebrities who appeared to share a cocktail at the bar were significant drawcards.

I envisioned almost cabaret French-style dancing with a touch of the Moulin Rouge thrown in for good measure, and I couldn't wait to show off my years of dancing talent and add a touch of sultry illusion. I knew I would be good to go when the velvet curtains parted for my moment in the spotlight.

What I was about to walk into was not even close to resembling what I envisioned, and my innocence was almost laughable. My interview was held in the afternoon, straight after I finished my shift at the library, which was no more than ten minutes down the road. I had no idea what attire would be appropriate for an interview in which the job in question required you to be wearing essentially nothing at all. After debating whether I should wear a bikini or a business dress, I decided a pair of smart dress pants and a button-down collared shirt would be a safe bet. After adding an extra amount of perfume and some shiny lip gloss, I walked into the doors of Zelda's for the first time.

It was a small club compared to what I had seen in movies. There was one large main stage with a pole and three separate podiums, each with poles in the middle, placed around a room that was covered in a dark-coloured velvet fabric. The velvet was the only hint of glamour. A large, leather-covered bar wrapped around one side of the room; bar stools were positioned to give patrons an unobstructed view of every stage and podium. That area of the bar led down to where the pool tables and extra chairs were placed. You stepped up to another level to sit in the matching velvety, rounded chairs that surrounded the main stage, and to your left, the upper level featured two cubicles with curtains that could be pulled across for privacy. These were explicitly for VIP lap dances. The main stage was also on the upper level and had an entrance from the dressing room off to one side and a DJ booth that stood at the back of the stage where the DJ or MC would play the same playlist night after night.

I couldn't help but notice the huge television screens that were placed along the edge of the ceiling. As it was daytime and the club was closed, the only clue to the wildness that took place each evening was the overwhelming smell of cigarettes and alcohol that had been spilt onto the plush seventies-style carpet for years.

I entrusted one girlfriend with the secret of what I was interviewing for, and she was both horrified and intrigued at the same time. She made me promise to tell her all the details the moment I left. She (and I) didn't really think I would go through with it. I had spent the past year being rather dull compared to other nineteen-year-olds. While the rest were doing body shots at night clubs, I had been having cups of tea, poring over books, and baking cupcakes at home. So, I was already in two minds before I walked in the door, but curiosity got the better of me, and I wanted to see what this other world was all about.

I was introduced to the owner, who wasn't as intimidating as I had imagined in my head. He was an older man who was very confident and had a look that told me he had most certainly seen it all before. He discussed how the club ran, explaining the rules he expected to be followed by both patrons and dancers and assuring me that it was strictly a 'no touching' club, which meant that the customers were not able to put their hands on you in any way. There was security in place to look after us, and on top of the hourly wage, we could keep all the tips we made, and there was no fee to be paid back to the club for dancing there.

It all sounded pretty straightforward, and with the ability to choose my own hours that could work around my schedule, I was definitely being swayed in the right direction. The owner made it clear during the interview that I could choose what level I wanted to play in my role within the club; I could simply serve drinks in the designated 'uniforms', I could dance on stage and on the poles while still covered up, or I could step it up and do nude sets and engage private lap dances. That sounded fine, and I liked the fact that I had control over how far I wanted to take it. At the end of the interview, he said he needed to make sure I would be confident working in the 'uniforms' that were available. He asked a young lady who was cleaning behind the bar to assist me in picking out something from the dressing room.

I must admit when the doors opened, it didn't resemble something from a Hollywood dressing room filled with fur, sequins, and taffeta wings. Instead, I found a rather reserved collection of outfits made up of skimpy G-strings and matching bikini tops. I was a little disappointed. I hunted through the velvet leopard print, red lace, and faux leather and settled on a beautiful blue lace set that—

except for the very tiny G-string portion—was exactly like something I would wear to the beach. Then came the infamous heels to match. I was given a new pair of black leather strappy heels that had a thick mirrored platform bottom and a sky-high mirrored stiletto point that looked almost impossible to even stand up in, but was genuinely impressive.

I managed to strap myself into the sky-scraping heels and changed into my lace ensemble. I took a few Bambi-like steps out of the dressing room door to do the required 360-degree reveal to the boss, and he declared, 'Perfect, though you could work on your tan. Ask the girls about the solarium they attend once you start.'

And just like that, I added 'stripper' to my resume.

I organised a friend of mine, Jessica, who worked at my son's daycare, to stay overnight twice a week at my house to watch Rhyz while I was at work. As my shift didn't start until 9 pm and finished at 2 am, I would still be there to put my son to bed and be safely back in my bed again by the time he woke in the morning. I would pay Jessica for babysitting throughout the evening, and she would sleep in the spare room that we had set up. Rhyz would never need to know I had even left the house. It was a perfect arrangement, and with my close friends sworn to secrecy about my new venture, I started my first shift the following Friday.

I was greeted at the door by Al, who introduced himself as the security guard and asked my name. 'I'm Angie,' I said, feeling quite nervous and overwhelmed by the loud music blasting from inside the wooden double doors.

He looked at me and with a quizzical expression, asked me, 'Is that your actual name?' I was confused and assured him it was. He clearly took sympathy on me at this stage and my naivety at the whole experience and told me, 'Choose a stage name, stick to it, and don't even tell the other girls what your real name is.'

He asked me what name I wanted to choose, and I swear that in that very moment, my whole creative side vanished and I instantly forgot every interesting name I had ever heard before.

'Um, Jess?' I said, already questioning how I was going to pull off an alter ego of alluring sexiness if I couldn't even manage a task as simple as choosing a name. He laughed and assured me it was going to be okay. He couldn't have been more than a couple of years older than me, but appeared to have worked there a while and knew his way around the business. He asked me to point out my car in the carpark beside the club so that he could keep an eye on it and told me he would be escorting me back to my car after my shift. If I needed him at any time during the evening to remove customers who weren't following rules, I simply had to come back to the door.

I thanked him and pushed through the wooden doors that opened instantly into sensory overload. The speakers around the room echoed obvious and corny 1980s stripper songs, the origin of which was a guy wearing a hat pulled down almost completely covering his eyes standing behind the DJ booth. I now saw what all those televisions were for, and I stood in disbelief as I took it all in; every screen showed different forms of retro porn movies being played in graphic high definition.

I tried to take it all in at once and at the same time, did my best not to look as shocked as I felt. I am not sure what I expected, but the reality of being face to—well—vagina with the girls standing directly in front of me on the podium was a little different to any room I had ever been in before.

There was a fast-moving girl behind the bar, and she was flat out serving drinks to fill the trays of other dancers who stood patiently with their work colleagues. They stood chatting and laughing in various stages of undress, before strutting off in their towering heels, balancing round black serving trays filled with drinks they had ordered on behalf of their customers. The girls all had bronzed skin glittering from the reflection of the various stage lights that shone around the room. Their faces were perfectly made up, their hair hung soft and loose around their shoulders, and they swung it seductively as they sauntered around. I was still standing in the doorway wearing my jeans and a singlet top, my new outfit tucked away in my handbag over my shoulder, still not quite sure what to do next. The girl behind the bar noticed me and called me over.

We introduced ourselves (I remembered to say my new name, Jess), and in between pouring cocktails into strange glass test tubes, she called over another dancer called Cherry (who had obviously spent more time being imaginative about her stage name) and asked her to show me the ropes. She was friendly and grabbed my hand as she led me through the crowded room of men aged from eighteen through to sixty who were dressed in everything from business attire to casual shirts and jeans. The air was thick with a mix of cigarettes, smoke machines, and high energy. The dressing room was bustling with dancers touching up their makeup, sharing a giggle about what was happening in the club that evening, and showing off their outfits. Everyone was kind; the surprising lack of bitchiness or competitiveness caught me off guard, and I made friends instantly.

They were right about being strict on the patrons, and if any overstepped the line by harassing or touching the dancers, they were instantly removed. It was a semi-safe environment which, while certainly not a high-class establishment by any means, was doing its part for the economy of the local community. The turnover of patrons ranged from your average tradies coming in with their mates after work to local politicians who came alone and sat quietly in the corner.

While I was very confident and not shy about my body as a teenager, it was certainly not easy to step up to the calibre of the feature performers who came through weekly. They were not only incredibly talented performers but were also in a different league to the average dancer. One particular young lady who I looked up to was a tiny blonde who went by the name Holly. Every couple of weeks she would appear with one small black travel suitcase on wheels, and in the dressing room, she would entirely make herself over with a flurry of hair curlers, a touch of blush, and the most delicate lingerie. Holly was secretly paying her way through university as she studied to be a doctor. The work hours suited her, and she only had to work a couple of hours a week to take home well over a thousand dollars in cash.

She never drank or hung around longer than necessary, though she always smiled and made polite small talk. For her, it was pure business, and I thought she was insanely clever. She used the ability she had to market herself well above everyone else to bring in significantly higher pay than an average dancer. The club would promote these 'feature performers' in the days leading up to their debut, and by the time they stepped their thigh-high leather stilettoed boots onto the main stage, the crowds would already be waving money in their direction. These ladies were intelligent; the exotic dance clubs would pay them a very high amount of money to do one set on stage, then if they chose to, they could name their price for VIP lap dances in the private cubicles.

One set typically consisted of three songs; the first song the dancer was fully clothed. The moment the second song hit, it was a cue for the dancer to remove her top, and the third song was danced entirely nude. Some dancers were experienced with doing acrobatics on the pole. Still, regardless of talent, flexibility, or looks, the girls with the personality and ability to connect with the patrons and their 'weak spot' were successful.

The majority of those who came in wanted a wild night with hot, young girls, and by gosh were we able to put on a show. But if you looked closer, you spotted those who wanted to brag about their work achievements, whinge about their home life, or just felt lonely and wanted to feel like someone was listening. Either way, the club paid us by the hour, and we relied heavily on the tips to bring in big money. If you were able to make a connection with someone and they enjoyed the small talk and had you taking their drink orders all night, more often than not they would tell you to buy yourself one and to keep the change, which worked out incredibly well for us as the club allowed us free drinks. If someone bought us a drink, we added it to the tab and got paid out at the end of the night for it. The customers were always informed of this but still told us to consider it an extra tip.

I knew of a few girls who would organise with the patrons to do private shows out of work time, and there were some pretty loud whispers regarding movies being made and distributed. From my position, I certainly didn't see any girls there who didn't want to be there. They certainly had many other options, but this one just happened to pay exceptionally well, so more power to them, I say.

I took advice from the other more experienced dancers and spent twice a week topping up my tan at the solarium, bearing in mind this was before they were illegal and before high-quality fake tan existed.

I also stopped wearing perfume or any glittery body creams so that it wouldn't be a drawback for patrons who didn't want to go home smelling like a teenager and looking like a fairy had dropped a glitter ball on them. I learnt the hard way that rubbing moisturising cream on your legs just before you take to the stage made it impossible to grasp the pole and it seriously makes for an awkward dance as you realise you are at high risk of flying off the stage if you lose balance on your heels.

Every person who walked through the door asked every dancer what their real name was, so we all had a second fake name. I, once again useless at thinking of a name on the spot, claimed it was 'Amy', which happened to be the name of another dancer in the club. My imagination never improved with experience.

As confident as I was, I wasn't able to be a feature dancer and I respected those who were so in touch with their own body that they could be that sensual on stage. I remember one night in particular that I was rewarded for holding my own. A gentleman had asked repeatedly for a VIP dance, but I was honest and said that I just didn't do them. His price kept rising, and I laughed him off and apologised and said I was more than happy to get his drink order, but I just wasn't going any further. He smiled and offered me $100 if I brought his drink back without my top on. I returned with his drink and my lace bikini top still in place, he smiled and placed $100 on my tray and looked at me, trying to read my face.

I told him I admired his determination, but I still wasn't taking my top off, and passed the cash back to him with the glass of rum. He laughed, winked at me, and pulled another $50 out of his wallet, and with the money I had just returned, passed me $150, saying that I was too smart for that place and hoped I had an exit strategy. I hugged him and said I most certainly did and that his money had just covered my power bill. I walked back to the dressing room to put it in my bag.

On average, I was able to take home in a night what it took me a week to earn at the university. I made sure that after I had paid my bills, I saved every dollar. I also managed to grow a pretty impressive collection of lingerie and held tight to the original mir-ror-bottom leather stilettos. I still have them hidden in the back of my cupboard.

I spent three months living a second life at night time, and it was a whole lot of fun. I saved a ton of money and made sure Rhyz and I had the financial security we needed. I kept it completely secret from everyone, except the few close friends who supported me through this time. One of the funniest moments would be when a club patron would come face-to-face with me on a Monday morning when they would come through the university library. Those moments were hilarious. They would start out with a look of confusion as they tried to figure out where they knew me, and it would transform into embar-rassment when they realised *exactly* why they were familiar with me.

I also cannot hear those first chords of Poison's 'Pour Some Sugar on Me' without instantly being transported right back into that strip club. It always makes me laugh to myself, certainly if it comes on the radio just before I am about to appear on stage at a professional event or I'm on the way to school drop off.

I had to sit my son down a couple of years ago when he was going through his own trials of teenage life, and he exclaimed in frustration that I wouldn't understand anything as life had always been so easy for me and I was so boring. At that stage, I realised just how well I had kept my past hidden, and it was probably the correct time to tell him that I am human, have lived a pretty interesting life, and I am most certainly far from perfect.

Back in those days, however, I was starting to worry. I wanted a serious career, and long-term employment that I could depend on that satisfied my intellectual drive. I wanted to continue to work or study my way up the career ladder.

Once again, it all began with a newspaper advertisement in the job vacancy section. By the time I was twenty, I was training and working as a full-time dental nurse. I had traded the stripper pole for scrubs, and I had unknowingly made one of the smartest long-term decisions that would assist me in setting myself up for success many times in my future.

CHAPTER 5

THESE DAYS

When I got the call to say I had been successful and given the position as a dental nurse, I squealed down the phone in excitement. It was a respected and well-paying career that I knew would be integral to building a future for my son and me. It most certainly wasn't an easy position, but years later it proved to be beneficial in setting me up for other significant business and career opportunities.

The dentist I would be training and working with was old fashioned, strict, and very intelligent. If I ever had to phone a friend on *Who Wants to Be a Millionaire*, it would have been him. He was an elderly gentleman from England who didn't tolerate any nonsense and would boast that in his entire career, spanning over forty years at that stage, he had only taken three sick days off.

He was what we called a 'wet-handed' dentist, which means that he often chose not to wear gloves during his treatment on patients but was strict that I was to use full gloves, mask, and all shields and barriers. The hours were long, and the starts were early, which took a bit of adjustment as the dental practice was thirty minutes away from home.

That meant I had to start my mornings from 6 am so I could share breakfast with Rhyz, then drop him off at daycare by 7.15 am each morning to make it to work by 7.45 am. I would start by setting up for the patients who began attending from 8 am. Most evenings would see me collect Rhyz from daycare again at 5.45 pm and then we would finally make it home by 6 pm, with enough time to shower, eat dinner, cuddle on the couch, and read a book together before falling into bed and starting it all again the next day. I had extra studies I completed at home during my early years, and I am not sure if it was the maternal guilt or the long hours that exhausted me more.

I can remember I specifically did not mention at my job interview that I had a child. I didn't want that to sway the decision making, and it was about eight months later that my boss overheard me mentioning to a patient that my son was also the same age as hers. After the patient left, he asked me why I hadn't told him I was a single mother. I replied a little defensively that it was because he hadn't asked me. He responded that if he had known, I would not have been given the position because children can cause a distraction in a career, but that it was too late now.

It was the only time I felt discriminated against for being a single mother in the workplace. I ignored his ignorant statement which, in this day and age, would be highly inappropriate. Back then, I was just grateful for the opportunity to have a career, and I kept quiet and made sure my home life never affected my work ethic.

While we were on a strict budget that allowed for Rhyz to enjoy his extra-curricular activities, it did mean that I had to make some sacrifices. In the middle of winter, our one heater would warm the lounge room, and then once Rhyz was put to bed, I would put the heater in his bedroom to keep him warm. I would then use the gas oven to heat the lounge room (it flowed from the adjoining kitchen), and then most nights I would crawl into my bed wearing a winter jacket over my pyjamas to stay warm.

Budgeting as a single mum was essential to keep our heads above water. My pay was a little above average, but with childcare and all the household bills to pay, there was very little left to save. As no financial advice was ever given to me, I chose to make budgeting so ridiculously simple that it has remained the same system for the rest of my future and it has served me well with budgeting and saving through the years. I used plain, old white envelopes with my expenses and amounts written on each: rent, petrol, groceries, daycare, power, etc. Each week, I put aside what was needed in the priority envelopes first and then I slowly added a little extra into a savings envelope to work towards something special.

My pride alone is what stopped me from being a stay-at-home mum and claiming government assistance. That, and I wanted to set a good example for my son and move myself up further in the world. I knew we could never buy a home if I didn't have a strong work history.

I wanted Rhyz to have many opportunities that came his way, and without any family support, I needed to work long hours. But sometimes I do look back and see that I was just struggling so badly to keep up with the constant workload. I remember some nights I would sit in the bottom of the shower and sob with sheer frustration and tiredness. *How would I ever know if I was making the right choices? What happened if something happened to me; who would look after my son?* I missed him when I was at work, and I felt so terrible that he spent more time at daycare than he did with me; it broke my heart. One evening, when I was putting Rhyz to bed and rubbing his back to soothe him to sleep, he asked me to pat his back instead, saying, 'Like daycare does, please.'

That hurt my soul greatly, and I always doubted if I was making the right choice. I'd be plagued by questions such as whether I was too focused on providing the support we needed that I was losing out on the important things in life.

These were the thoughts that kept me up at night. Those first few years were the hardest. I suffered terribly with guilt and always felt as though I wasn't doing enough or being present enough in the few hours a day we spent together. I didn't know how I would change our circumstances for me to be able to afford cutting back to a part-time job, but I knew that if I just kept pushing forward, surely it would pan out somehow. But the uncertainty of when and how that would happen left me feeling depressed at times. *Am I doing enough? Am I covering every aspect of securing my son's future happiness and security? Who do I turn to for advice?* I never wanted my son to feel the loneliness I did, and I tried so hard to fill his life with many adventures and happy moments so that he would never notice he was missing out on an extended family.

I was too scared to reach out and ask for help from a doctor or medical specialist to assist me. I never wanted to let anyone know that I couldn't cope. The fear from my past and the fact I was now a single mother kept me masking my deep sadness and anxiety from even those closest to me.

I would allow myself to fall apart once I had my son sleeping soundly in bed, so he never had to witness what I classed as my weakness. I felt I couldn't trust anyone to know just how much I struggled to even get out of bed in the mornings. I didn't ever want to lose my son, to be locked up in a psychiatric ward without control again, and I certainly didn't want the stigma of being medicated. I was afraid, and I spent the early years of my twenties having to draw on everything I had left inside me just to keep going.

I was making headway in securing a niche career when we began working in private hospitals with surgeons, performing bone grafting and dental implants, which weren't as commonly done by a general dentist twenty years ago. My role at the surgery, on top of dental nursing, was also to run the reception, do all invoicing, banking, and the processing of x-rays in the small darkroom we had beside the office. It gave me a fantastic all-round experience that showed me how a business ran and the aspects behind it, plus the workload it takes to make a business successful. Having a dental surgery run by just the nurse and the dentist meant there was no chance of having any time off. All my holidays were paid as I earned them. This meant each six months I received two weeks' holiday pay on top of my usual wage. This worked out brilliantly as it allowed me to ensure we had extra money, both mid-year for Rhyz's birthday and at Christmas, to celebrate with. I also had regular pay rises which allowed me to embark on some exciting adventures.

The first on my list was to take a holiday back home to Queensland. This time, I would be able to save enough money to stay in a hotel and enjoy the long-awaited reunion with some wonderful old school friends who had been instrumental in quelling my loneliness during quiet nights at home with phone calls that went for hours. I still spoke to Luke regularly, and we had been cheering and encouraging each other on for the past few years. Regardless of whether we had partners, we always had time for each other. It was almost a protective friendship between us, and I couldn't wait to see him and our mutual friends. Sam, who I had been best friends with since primary school, had also found himself a girlfriend called Trina, and I was pumped to meet up with them all.

I was thrilled when I finally booked the flights. I had spent three months slowly paying off the hotel accommodation fees in advance, and with my twenty-first birthday freshly celebrated, I couldn't contain my excitement at spending seven days with those closest to me.

A couple of months before my flight, Luke called bursting with good news, and I still remember exactly where I was when he told me. I was standing under the huge tree in the Queens Street courtyard in Fremantle, in front of my work, on my lunch break when he exclaimed that he had just bought a house with his girlfriend. I think I was speechless for the first few minutes and managed to tell him just how wonderful that was and congratulate him wholeheartedly before making up an excuse and getting off the phone quickly. It stung. The feeling of that stabbing chest pain came right out of nowhere. I had no explanation for it whatsoever.

At the time, I was also in a happy relationship with a guy who I had been dating, and I had never previously felt any pangs of jealousy at all relating to Luke since we broke up over seven years earlier. We had remained so close for so many years, and this feeling came out of the blue. I dismissed it as just an emotional day, and I managed to not think about it again. I looked forward to celebrating his great achievement when I arrived to see his new home.

The trip was the first since I had attempted to return almost five years earlier, and the reunion with everyone was better than I could have imagined. I had found a new best friend in Sam's partner, Trina, the instant I met her (spoiler alert: they are still together and happily married almost fifteen years later!) and when I opened the door to Luke at the hotel, time stood still again for a split second. We had a fantastic night with a big group of us reminiscing and laughing, and I felt like that missing part of me was whole again for a moment. My homesickness was relieved. It took until the early hours for Luke to admit that his partner was no longer in his life and we organised to spend the next few days together chilling at his new home and catching up on everything that we hadn't already shared on our long phone calls.

Luke opened up and explained there had been some issues in their relationship regarding jealousy about our tight-knit friendship. I understood. I also had spent time convincing my partner that Luke and I had a genuinely platonic friendship, and there was no risk of crossing over in the separate lives we had intentionally built. There may have been a moment that we shared a laugh over this topic and our eyes met just for that little bit too long with this strange feeling behind them, but I put that down to the extra glasses of wine we had drunk and thought no more of it. It was hard to get back on the plane and leave it all behind again. But I had work to get back to, and my son was beginning school soon, so I returned to the other side of Australia.

When I arrived home, I noticed that maybe there was a connection missing. When I stared into the eyes of my partner, it didn't have that spark that Luke and I did. Although Luke and I were just friends, I realised that a long term partner of mine was going to at least need to have that same basis of soul recognition that we shared. I decided that I was going to remain single until I met someone who made my heart skip a beat. I chose to end the relationship and resumed my focus on balancing my routine of work, life, and motherhood.

I will freely admit I was not a perfect girlfriend back then. I'd keep my partner at arm's length and was wary of letting my guard down. I still tend to hold most people at a distance; it is a purely self-protective mechanism that kicked in years ago and has never left. However, I do believe I just wasn't emotionally mature enough to be a good girlfriend at that time in my life. I thought I was confident and self-assured, but looking back, I was still constantly worried I was not good enough, and no-one would want me to build a life with me.

I think I was stretched thin with putting my son first, and after my workload, I didn't have enough left in me to give to anyone else. I wish at the time I had realised this. I didn't know how to maintain a relationship, and it resulted in good people being hurt due to my defensive behaviour. As much as I would love to paint a picture of 'poor me', I am sure at times I was a selfish and hurtful partner who didn't know how to communicate and insisted on focusing solely on my son's and my needs, and that embarrasses me greatly. I just didn't know how else to have a relationship where I trusted the person implicitly. I would cut ties if I felt the relationship was getting too serious, which hurt their feelings and left me looking cruel.

I am not too sure what it was that started to unhinge me slightly, but I think the pressures of parenting alone and long work hours were beginning to take their toll on me and I struggled to keep up with it all. I very rarely went out, and my social life was back to being non-existent, which was fine as Rhyz filled my weekends with trips to the movies, swimming lessons, and various sporting activities. But that feeling like something was missing continued to follow me around for months. I was lonely for something I couldn't quite put my finger on, and I couldn't find a way to fill the empty feeling.

As a very last minute decision, I bought a plane ticket home again to Queensland for a two-night stay. Leaving just after Boxing Day, I once again relished the feeling of belonging among the company of my friends. Luke and I spent every moment together, laughing at how the ring I had given him nearly a decade ago was now permanently stuck on his finger, and we drank and spoke about life. We may have drunk a little too much. After all those years being best friends, he opened up, expressing how he had never stopped loving me and that his past relationships had all been affected because of this. As I looked into the eyes of the first boy who ever held my heart, I knew I felt exactly the same way. Suddenly we had both drawn closer and almost as soon as his lips brushed mine, I felt myself panic. *What was happening? Luke was the only person who had never let me down, and I can't do this. I will ruin it, I will close down, and then I won't have anyone in the universe left in my corner, as he had always been. I couldn't lose that; I couldn't lose him.*

Now the story between us differs greatly. He insisted that I, at first, kissed him back. I had always refuted this version. However, the ending was always the same; I pulled away, and I slapped him. Hard. Right across the face. I asked him to leave immediately.

He said later that as he drove away he was still in total shock about what had just happened and how it went so wrong. I spent the evening in shock and almost frozen, not knowing what on earth was going to happen next. I couldn't lose him, but we couldn't be together. We were divided by an entire country, and of all the things I could live without, his friendship in my life wasn't one on them. He meant too much. There were a few weeks of silence between us after I arrived back in Western Australia. Once the communication opened up again, we made light-hearted jokes about it and resumed the close friendship we had maintained throughout the years.

They say when you are not actively looking for something, that is most likely the time it will arrive unannounced on your doorstep. What happened next was a perfect example of this.

Some of my friends had been trying for a long time to get me to be more social, and I knew I needed to get out in the world more, so when an invitation arrived to attend a friend's birthday party at a high-end venue, I didn't need too much convincing.

I still remember the red dress with the lace back that I wore as I stepped into a circle of new faces who had all come together to celebrate this special occasion. The music in the casino nightclub pumped heavily in the background and glasses of champagne were handed around to toast with and introduce ourselves. The moment I locked eyes with Dylan, and we matched smiles with each other, it was as though the entire room cleared out and the music ceased to exist. We grinned broadly at each other as we raised our glasses to toast cheers to the evening, and without us knowing, it was clear to the whole room that there was undeniable instant chemistry between us.

He had a way about him that was quietly confident, and his eyes that lit up the room when he laughed. Dylan was seven years my senior and I thought he was just mesmerising.

We spent the next six hours by each other's side as though we had known each other in a past life, and we danced and talked until the sun came up. He worked away in the mines in a fly-in fly-out job that saw him away for three weeks and home for one. There was little phone coverage out there, but when he asked for my number upon leaving, we agreed to keep in touch.

He was in my every waking thought from the moment I laid eyes on him. His thick, shaggy hair that had sun-bleached ends curling softly around his ears, and his deep tan from years spent living close to the ocean just added to his rugged handsomeness.

Within the next three months, we saw each other for maybe a week in total during the time that he was back from his shifts, and when he was away we had sporadic phone conversations that lasted into the early hours of the morning.

Dylan made me feel alive. He looked at me like I was the most beautiful girl he had ever seen, hanging on to my every word. I just basked in his glow and thought he was breathtaking. He was hard-working, independent, and successful, and I cannot even comprehend how much I adored him. Swept up in the romance of two old souls who both had always dreamed of fairytales and the rush of finding our soulmates, we allowed ourselves to fall head over heels in love. Looking back, maybe it was lust, or—even more straightforward—the *idea* of love. We would talk about our deepest secrets, the incredible dreams we had for the future, and all the adventures we were going to share. It was like a bolt of lightning had hit me; the excitement and the passion between us was magic.

We would slow-dance around the lounge room late at night, hearts bursting with passion and just staring adoringly at one another. *This must be what true love feels like*, I thought to myself.

Dylan waited until his third trip home and then expressed his absolute devotion on one knee with the most insane two-carat tanzanite ring I had ever seen, leaving me breathless and beside myself with joy. With him having to leave for another three-week work stint the very next morning, we sprinted to a twenty-four-hour police station in Fremantle and had them witness our hastily prepared intention-to-marry forms.

The next week at work, I told my boss I needed to take a day off for a medical appointment in a month. Without telling his family, our friends, or anyone else, the man I had met only three months earlier and had spent approximately seven days in total with, held my hands as we stood in front of a celebrant on a secluded beach and declared our everlasting love for one another. I wore a white silk, flowing, halter-neck gown with a crystal waist and crystal-covered veil that swept around my feet, with my new husband accessorising his expensive suit with black Oakleys® and a proud smile. At the age of twenty-two, I married for the second time.

CHAPTER 6

TEARS DRY ON THEIR OWN

How I wish I could write this chapter by painting myself in a good light. Unfortunately, I have no-one to blame but myself for the mess that occurred. Newly married, I decided it was time to step out of my comfort zone in all areas and take a risk by moving to a new dental practice that was considerably larger, more modern, and also closer to home.

That was one of the most intelligent moves I made that year as it allowed me to work my thirty-eight hours in a four-day week, giving me a much-needed day off with my son mid-week to spend more quality time with him. My maternal guilt started to ease slightly (I am not sure if it ever really goes away though. He is about to turn twenty, and it is still there from time to time). I was able to move once again to a higher pay grade and start learning orthodontic nursing techniques that I could add to my resume down the track. I was surrounded by the most incredible work colleagues. They went on to become lifelong friends. This made attending work every day an absolute pleasure, and I loved being part of such a professional team.

My career was taking off again, my son was going brilliantly at school and excelling at his weekend soccer games, and my marriage—well, that was another story. Ten years ago, I would have said the issues we faced were entirely Dylan's fault, but I am not sure that is true anymore.

It is funny what time does. It lessens the anger, or the pain felt in the moment, and allows you to see the situation through clearer eyes. I also think as you grow older emotionally, you can own the parts of you that were lacking in the past.

We decided it would be easier for Dylan to move in with us to keep the family home for Rhyz so that his needs were put first. Sadly, I didn't realise how much defiance Rhyz would feel towards Dylan. Before Dylan moved in with us, Rhyz had been pretty blasé about his presence, but his attitude went from noncommittal to intense discomfort the moment Dylan's bags were unpacked. They couldn't seem to find common ground or a way to connect.

Initially, I put that down to just needing a little more time to adjust to our lifestyle, but I was also keenly aware that we had rushed into this without allowing Rhyz to be more confident of the new family structure. Dylan, on the other hand, had also decided to follow his passion and change his career. After working away for so many years, he found his dream job not far from our home to settle into within a few weeks of our marriage. For a little while there we were celebrating following our dreams. We were going to be each other's cheerleader as we moved forward in the world together. This didn't last for too long, though.

Only within a couple of weeks of our legal everlasting expressions of devotion, the cracks started to show. We didn't have enough time to get to know each other properly beforehand (no surprises there). Instead of basing our relationship on a solid foundation of friendship, it was built on excitement, lust, and spontaneity.

I remember meeting his family for the first time, and because we had eloped, the reaction was less than welcoming. As I stood beside my new husband at one of his family member's wedding receptions, I felt tears run down my face as intoxicated relatives took great pride in throwing random things at my back and laughing as they bounced off my head. I could hear them cackling, and as I tried to draw Dylan's attention to it, he just told me to stop taking it so seriously, and they were just having some fun. Their fun soon turned to open cruelty when they took turns making crude comments about what type of woman I was to their brother to 'earn' the big rock on my finger, and they laughed as I blushed uncomfortably at their lack of any sensitivity. I soon realised that his family was certainly not going to be opening their arms to our relationship. Having the only brother in a large family of sisters running off and eloping before anyone had even met his new wife was a transgression that was not going to be forgiven lightly.

The expressions of him being a family man and my ideas of what that entailed were very separate things. There was no friendship at all between my son and Dylan. His idea of spending time together as a family was doing all the bachelor things he used to do that appeased his needs but didn't allow for a family lifestyle we would all enjoy together. Weekends were spent with us waiting on his return from outings with his friends on boats or four-wheel-drive trips instead of being the active parent that I guess I expected, but did not have the ability to express to him. He remained absent both physically and emotionally; the situation soon became a mess of miscommunication and disappointment on my behalf.

He was up for displays of romantic affection and grandiose gestures such as asking a jeweller to open after hours at the Perth Casino so he could buy me yet another elaborate ring. He would bring home bouquets so large that they would only fit in the laundry tub. Yet he was unable to be home for Christmas Eve, choosing to spend it with his friends instead of his family, which made for a very conflicted environment.

I realised that while his intentions towards me were initially true, we hadn't worked out how to become a family, and that was the part I valued the most. Suddenly, I felt entirely trapped. Instead of welcoming his over-the-top expressions of love, I felt more and more claustrophobic, as though I had made a rash decision, and it was the wrong one. Now, I didn't trust anything I felt. *How could I have gotten it so wrong again?* I badly wanted a family, but what I had was a husband, and those two things aren't necessarily the same thing.

I resorted to the only way I knew how to react and started to retreat into myself, not only distancing myself emotionally but physically as well. I became angry and resentful because I didn't have control over the future again, and I so desperately wanted the fairytale to come true. I know I wasn't the easiest person to be with at this point; I swung between pushing him away and being overly needy. At the time I felt it was all justified, years later I imagine he was just as angry and resentful too. We both wanted this, and then we couldn't make it work. It was a very depressing time filled with tension and confusion.

While we had realised we worked well side by side, we certainly didn't know how to make life work together as a family unit. I hadn't experienced this before, and the fact I was already struggling with my own emotions before we married meant I wasn't even sure how I would go about communicating this with him without coming across like a very ungrateful partner.

Without the prior friendship to build from, we couldn't find a way to work well together once the novelty of all the romantic gestures had worn off.

I can remember at the time honestly believing I was trying my hardest to bring back that connection we had felt so strongly, yet I couldn't recover it—from either of us. Almost as fast as we fell in love (if that is what it was), we were strangers sharing a house.

As it is me who is writing this book, and it leaves no room for Dylan to give his side of the story, I am going to wear this mistake personally. It is not fair to paint someone wholly in a bad light when he is not available to able to provide his version.

What I do know is it was apparent to us both quite quickly that rushing into this may not have been our brightest idea. The romantic nights of talking until the sun came up were replaced by deafening silence. It was as though each of us had changed the instant the marriage papers were filed.

It was within the first two months he had already succumbed to packing his bags and leaving one night to have a breather from the tension that was circulating my home. For me, that was it. It didn't matter what happened throughout the next few months as we went back and forth, attempting to keep it together. The relationship limped along sadly with many nights spent apart, and I sobbed myself to sleep most nights as I felt like I had proved the inevitable: *I am truly unlovable, and maybe I don't even have a real soulmate.* For the great romantic that was hidden deep within me, this was a gut-wrenching thought.

I so badly wanted a big family of my own—a place where I felt I always belonged—and I wanted that for Rhyz more than anything. The poor child had asked for a brother every year for Christmas, even when I was single. I used to joke that I couldn't find one amongst the cauliflowers at the shopping centre. The dream of giving him a sibling seemed more distant than ever, and I felt like I had let him down again as I watched my second marriage crumble before my eyes.

I was at work when the practice manager called me into her office and told me Dylan was on the phone; she looked concerned. I had no idea what to expect as I hadn't seen him in the days prior as he had once again packed his bags and left after we had a disagreement, refusing to answer the phone when I tried to reach out to him.

When I hung up the phone, I couldn't stop the tears from falling, and I sat on the floor in my boss's office, hidden from patients in the waiting room, knowing at that exact moment movers were taking my husband's belongings from my home. It was all over. My dear colleague and best friend, Tanya, swept me into the bathrooms and held me as I cried, positive my heart was surely breaking.

I came home to find his wedding ring left on the bench. No other trace of his existence was to be found. We never had to worry about dividing the property as he had taken half of everything, which he was rightly entitled to, but certainly to the point of pettiness. Half the cutlery set was taken, one bedside dresser, saucepans, even a poster that was bought to hang on Rhyz's wall had been removed as his bank card had been used to purchase it.

I sat on the cold slate floors of my kitchen with Tanya beside me, and I tried to take it all in. My second marriage hadn't even lasted a year.

Any remainder of dignity I had was gone, and I took a week off from work to try to pull myself together. That was a slow slide into a depression where I really couldn't find my feet. I was so lucky to have such a supportive team of colleagues who held me up and helped me through such a low time. They did what all wonderful girlfriends do when things go pear-shaped and arrived on my doorstep with food and drinks, insisting on movie nights and family days out together. I am not sure if they knew how much they kept my head up during that time. I was, and am, so grateful for them. They were my crutch for the next year as I tried to rebuild my confidence, and they stood by me as I continued once again to attempt to find my spot in the world.

What happened next was something I never intended to write about, as I will seem like one of those characters in movies that you scream at through the television screen in an attempt to tell them they are about to do something entirely stupid.

I considered just glossing over it as it would, firstly, paint me in a better light; secondly, make me appear as strong as I wished I had been during this time, and finally, save me a lot of embarrassment from admitting I must have been a total train wreck by this stage in my life.

But I am far from perfect, and this is real life, so here goes: the year following the separation from my husband, I continued to battle insomnia and anxiety, which was beginning to be evident to those around me. I had developed a stutter that made me hugely self-conscious, and I began to experience panic attacks, which hadn't happened to me since my teens. Once again, instead of reaching out for help, I sat in silence and suffered alone.

As hard as I tried to move on physically, emotionally, I was falling apart inside. My stress levels rose, and my professionalism at work declined rapidly. I could hardly sleep at night, insomnia haunted me and added to my despair. I must have slept through my alarm a handful of times, making me late to my shifts and putting pressure on the rest of the team to pick up my slack. I was distracted at work and so tired from lack of sleep that I recall even falling asleep during my lunch break in the staff room. Finally, after a few warnings, my boss gave me the news that I was dismissed from my position, explaining that I just wasn't working to the professional level that I previously had, which was required in my job. It was understandable, and the fact they had supported me through the toughest times during my marriage breakdown was already going above and beyond what any employer would normally do. But now my fall from grace was complete. It was the final straw of humiliation for me. It was the first job I had ever been fired from, and I couldn't seem to do anything right that year as I let myself down more than I possibly could have let anyone else down.

After many years of no communication or having a relation-ship with my mother, I chose that moment to reach out for some help. I was at such a low point and didn't know what to do next. I think there was a high chance I had already hit my emotional rock bottom and the subsequent few weeks, while I tried to mend broken bridges between my mother and me, felt like being dragged across that rocky bottom, tearing myself and the remaining pieces of my life to shreds.

I think some things can never be salvaged, and when I reached out to my mother for the first time in years, the fact that some things can never change was cemented, regardless of time or situation, and this was my new low. I allowed her to know that I had failed, and instead of me being swept up and cared for in the way only a mother can do, I ended up feeling as though I had made an even bigger mistake by trying with her again. After some excruciatingly painful attempts between us to heal some very old and still very raw wounds, it became apparent that there was no relationship between us and none would ever be formed in the future.

I reached out to Luke, as we had continued to support each other through all the ups and downs that life threw our way. There were obvious signs over the past decade that we had a stronger connection than just best friends. Regardless of whether we had partners or what we were doing in life, we always prioritised each other first, much to the chagrin of whoever our poor, long-suffering partners were at the time.

However, this time was different. When my marriage fell apart, Luke was supportive, but I could feel the distance in his voice when we would speak. I had run off and eloped with someone after he had tried to express his feelings to me, resulting in the aforementioned slap to his face that he never let me live down.

It was at this time our friendship would change forever and not in the right way. I was angry at the world, and he was sick of me changing my mind every two seconds; one moment agreeing that we were soulmates and the next declaring that I wasn't too sure and then choosing a virtual stranger to marry instead.

One night, after hours on the phone going back and forth about who had done what wrong and why it wouldn't work, the conversation turned heated. He had waited years for me to come back and stood beside me as I rejected his affections and toyed with his emotions; he was upset and had every right to be. Luke had previously said he would get a plane ticket and come over, and he had been looking at airfares, but this last phone call, he said he couldn't do it. He was tired of waiting on me to make up my mind, tired of always being the one there and me not caring until I needed him.

He was right, but this time my apologies weren't enough. He had tried since we were fourteen years old to convince me that we were soulmates, and he was tired of it all. It hurt him to watch as I chose to stay away, and I hurt from feeling so lost; I couldn't lose him too. He didn't see it that way, and he finally had enough. I don't recall the exact words that were said but tears and yelling were involved and suddenly for the first time since we were twelve years old the phone was slammed down for the last time. The silence in the seemingly endless years that followed was deafening.

I swore to myself this was it. I needed to pull myself together, and I had to do nothing but shut out the world and focus on the positives (which I had yet to find, other than my beautiful son). I had to forget about the pain that losing my marriage, job, and friendship with Luke brought into my soul when I was unable to sleep late at night.

I was going to turn my life around and crawl my way back from the hole I had managed to fall into. I got into my car with my wedding dress and photos and delivered them straight to the dump, feeling a sense of satisfaction as I heard the glass frames shatter in the cement pit below. On the way home, I ceremoniously threw my wedding band into the river, and by the week's end, I had organised my divorce papers, signed them, and had them served to Dylan.

By the end of the month, I was determined to stop merely surviving and to start succeeding again.

CHAPTER 7

HIGH HOPES

With a new drive, I refused to put myself back down in that hole again. I decided to focus on my health for the first time in a long time, and I made sure to put myself alongside Rhyz at the top of my priority list. I secured a new job within weeks, and this time I was able to negotiate the hours around my son's school day, meaning I had just enough time to drop him at school and collect him and there was no more before or after school care needed in our lives.

I thought moving house would provide us with an opportunity to feel like we had something that was just ours again and would allow us some control back of our lives. We found a small beach-type shack in a quiet neighbourhood, and Rhyz and I started to piece together our life all over again. I had moved us thirty minutes away from our previous home in Rockingham to Fremantle to cement a proper fresh start in a new environment, and it was filled instantly with a vibe of hope and happiness.

Before long, our new house was filled with our furniture, and we were able to start doing things together that we never had the luxury of doing before, like joining after-school sports teams for

Rhyz because my work hours were no longer so overwhelming. He excelled at cricket and Little Athletics, and I cheered him on proudly from the sidelines. He was able to have friends over after school as I was no longer at work in the evenings, and our cosy home was filled with lots of small feet running around. I finally felt the balance come back into our lives that had been missing for so long.

We had a small two-bedroom house on a large block with a huge backyard, and although it wasn't fancy in any way, it brought us so much joy. We spent our spare time attending car shows, which had become a passion I had inherited from my dad, and regularly wandered around the Fremantle markets on a Sunday. In my kitchen, I would bake to my heart's content. The pressure seemed to have lifted, work became less overwhelming, and I was able to prioritise time with my son, which was really what made my heart happy.

I was working in the heart of Fremantle, which is a beautiful town, and I was lucky to work alongside a colleague who became a lifelong friend called Ali. It was the first time I had found the right balance in life, and I genuinely loved heading in to work. I spent my time in between work commitments chatting with Ali about the real important things in life, such as where we would go if there was a zombie apocalypse, and discussing world affairs and history. Life had a really good feeling about it, and I definitely felt I had found my groove.

I had finally met some other parents at the school after so many years of not being available to attend events, and now I had a few friends who I could have a cup of coffee and a laugh with when our children played after school. It was nice to belong somewhere again, and I started to realise for the first time that other mothers struggled to balance it all at times too. That knowledge alone made me feel so much more secure in myself. I still thought about Luke but resisted the temptation to reach out again. Instead, after months of searching, I found a gold and diamond forget-me-not ring online, exactly like the one he had given me at fourteen. Without ever telling anyone its significance, I put it back on and wore it daily to keep his memory close. The original one was sold at a pawn shop when I was with Nick to buy newborn nappies and a nappy bag all those years earlier, so I knew it wasn't the same one, but it seemed to bring me comfort, even if I did miss him dreadfully.

I decided to start up my almost forgotten bucket list again, and I began learning to play acoustic guitar with weekly lessons. Although I sadly had no hidden talent in the area, I enjoyed it immensely. I joined a Lindy Hop swing dance class and relished in all the happiness that had been injected into our lives. I felt fantastic in my tiny circle of life and safe in the zone that I had created. Rhyz and I were back to a weekend movie or bowling dates, and after a few months, all felt good in the world again.

My anxiety, panic attacks, stutter, and insomnia had disappeared, and I took pleasure in settling into bed each night with cups of tea and a thick book or a good movie.

I was around twenty-five years old at that time, and due to all of my hard work, I still hadn't needed to be supported on a government pension or have any debt. I made a choice that I would get a second job to start making moves towards buying my first home. I was still happily single and had been then for the best part of two years, and I enjoyed it immensely. I had never been happier in my life, and I still look back at this point in my history as one of the most blissful times when I felt truly content.

To find a second job, I had to come across something that didn't interfere with my day job or my quality time with Rhyz. I found the perfect option when I applied to work in a large Irish pub on the main cappuccino strip of Fremantle called Rosie O'Grady's. I was excited to begin my one-night-a-week roster as it involved working with the friendliest group of people I had met in a long time. Rosie's wasn't a small venue; it was a prominent feature that stood proudly in the centre of the street with huge balconies overlooking the nightlife below. Downstairs was where the main action happened. There were two large bars right next to a stage where popular cover bands played live music and filled the dance floor. It had a large restaurant on the opposite side of the vast room and upstairs featured private event rooms with bars, and there was accommodation available as well.

It was infamous in Fremantle, and I recall one of my most favourite shifts, which saw the final hurrah of a hugely popular local band. The crowd screamed the songs all night, the singer launched himself up onto the rafters and swung himself over the crowded dance floor. It was a brilliant place to work. My colleagues were mainly backpackers, travellers, or students, and their stories of adventures and experiences were the highlights of my week. I learnt how to pour a good Guinness, met a new circle of friends, and once a week when our shift was over, a group of us would change out of our work shirts and head down the street to a nightclub called The Clink where we would dance, laugh, and have a few drinks together.

A manager at Rosie's had asked me out a couple of times, but I was quite open in my reluctance to date anyone. I was sure I had inherited what my dad had called being a '2,000 miler' which meant I would surely attract any idiot within 2,000 miles. Finally, after a few months, I caved and agreed to go on a date with him. His name was Ben, and he had just landed in Perth after travelling the world from his hometown in Wodonga, in country Victoria. He was loud, funny, and the kindest person I have ever met to this day. He was friends with everyone and the quintessential Aussie larrikin with a heart of gold. Ben and I were instant friends from the time I started work at Rosie's.

I took the blossoming relationship very slowly. We got to know each other really well, and I was very open about my nervousness about getting hurt again, or worse, having my son disappointed and let down. Ben was incredibly understanding and supportive; he knew that I was very hesitant to introduce anyone to my son and waited patiently until the time was right. I thought maybe the best way would be to start slowly by including Rhyz and Ben at group activities such as the barbecues and beach days organised by the work crew at Rosie's so that they could get acquainted in a neutral, non-obvious way.

The next step was to wait a few months after that. We planned to sit him down and explain we would like to start seeing each other, therefore making it appear as though it was an involved decision and hopefully make Rhyz feel secure with our relationship.

We decided after about four months of dating and working together that I would bring Rhyz along to a beach cricket match held by the Rosie's crew and let Rhyz slowly get to know everyone. There must have been at least twenty of us on Fremantle Beach that afternoon. We had discussed with everyone the prior week that Rhyz wasn't aware of us dating and we would like to keep it that way for a while. Everyone was aware of our request.

It was a hot summer day, and while a large group played on the grass, others sat around drinking ciders and providing a running commentary of the game as it happened.

Rhyz, always a confident young fellow, was now ten years old, and he quickly asked the older guys if he could have a go. He spent the next hour having the time of his life, batting and bowling to his heart's content. When it was his turn to catch, he wandered instantly over to Ben in the outfield, and I watched, in suspense, from the sidelines with the others as he reached his little hand out to introduce himself and shook his hand. They then stood side by side for at least another hour laughing and talking nonstop and doing a rather dismal job of catching anything that was thrown in their direction. I was dying to know what was being said and why Rhyz had chosen Ben to shadow all afternoon.

It wasn't long after the sun started to go down and people began to walk back to the sidelines that Rhyz made a beeline directly for me, his long tanned legs walking faster the closer he got, and once he stood straight in front of me, he asked, 'Mum, I've met Ben, and he's really nice. Can he come back to our house for fish and chips tonight?' I felt twenty pairs of eyes staring at me as I stumbled and tried to pretend this wasn't the big deal that it clearly was.

I acted nonchalantly and said, 'Sure. He can come if he likes.' Rhyz raced back to ask his new friend over for dinner. Smiles lit up everyone's knowing faces, and they all innocently pretended this was a minor happening and off we went, back to our house for dinner, where Rhyz and Ben spent the rest of the evening talking a mile a minute about their shared interests. Ben left at bedtime, and we waved each other goodbye as the friends we were pretending to be and grinned to each other at just how easy this had gone.

As I tucked Rhyz into bed that night, he told me that he liked Ben and I should have a boyfriend like him as he wanted to see him again. I am not sure if we ever told Rhyz we were already dating for months prior; we just started to see more of each other, much to Rhyz's delight, and he was thrilled to have Ben come around. Over dinner one night, Ben mentioned his rental property was being sold, and he needed to move out. Without missing a beat, Rhyz said, 'Well why don't you move in here with us?' and that is how Ben moved in and became part of the family.

Our house became filled with more laughter, and Rhyz's confidence skyrocketed. He wanted to spend every moment with Ben, and in return, Ben instantly fell in love with this young boy who idolised him. Not long after Ben moved in, he asked me to marry him, and Rhyz squealed even louder than I did. Our small family celebrated together, and once again, I was engaged. I felt no hesitation; Ben was a gentleman who my son adored with every inch of his being, and I had waited nearly a decade for a man to come into my life who made my son smile as he did.

Ben spent his spare time making pizzas with Rhyz and showing him how to play games and was sincerely excited to be part of my family of two. He made me happy, and he made me laugh. We were friends first, which was such an essential step in building our family. He got along with Rhyz as though they were each other's shadows and we all loved being together. This time it was going to be wonderful, and I felt content with my life.

Ben had his flights booked to travel home to spend Christmas with his family and was planning on telling them the big surprise news of our engagement then. However, just a few days into his trip, I discovered there was a bigger surprise than initially expected—I was pregnant with our first child.

We were elated, as was his wonderful family, and Rhyz couldn't contain his joy. We sat around the lounge one night on Ben's return, and Rhyz asked in a timid and shaky voice if he would be allowed to call Ben 'Dad' too. I don't know who cried harder out of the three of us, as my little boy beamed with pride at the role model he had always wanted. Not long after this, I discovered he had taken to every school book and crossed out his surname and changed it to match Ben's. He was so excited and proud that we never mentioned to him that legally he wouldn't be able to do that. To him, it was so important that he even asked his teachers to change his name on the roll and class photos, which they did, bless them.

With a new baby on the way, we started to make all these grand plans. First off, we would need a bigger home as we needed a bit of space to add a nursery. We found the ideal home not far from where we were with the perfect nursery room that adjoined the master bedroom. It was also close to Rhyz's bedroom, which was a top priority for him, as he finally was getting his wish of becoming a big brother. We put the wedding plans on hold until after the birth and started picking out baby names. We had an ultrasound picture done when I was about nine weeks along and hung it above our bed. I would often find Ben and Rhyz staring at the little 'jelly bean' in the photo trying to guess if it was a boy or a girl.

We were hoping we might get lucky and find out the sex at the next ultrasound, which I had booked at thirteen weeks. We took Rhyz out of school early that day, and I got leave from my day job. With bets taking place on whether he was getting a brother or a sister, we practically levitated with excitement into the ultrasound room at the hospital. We told the sonographer what we each guessed it was going to be; Ben thought a girl for sure, and Rhyz and I insisted it was to be a little boy. We knew it wasn't common to know so early, but we were all hoping it might just give us a glimpse. She smiled at our delight as she started the scan, and I watched her as she worked the doppler around my lower stomach, and I stared at the screen, waiting to see what she said. Rhyz and Ben sat on chairs on either side and kept pointing out images on the screen asking if that was a foot or asking which way 'Jellybean' was facing.

The sonographer was doing a lot of measuring and didn't really respond. She asked us to wait for a second as she needed someone else to give her some assistance. She left the room, and the colour on my face drained at the same time. I had this instant horrible feeling that something was wrong.

When she returned with a colleague, they went through the same scanning procedure again together in silence and then turned and announced that I would need to head up to a private hospital not far away to have something checked. They would call ahead, and we would be seen immediately. I kept asking if everything was okay and the sonographer confirmed they just needed a second opinion. My whole body suddenly felt foreign, and I remember hardly breathing so that I could listen because a feeling of pure cold fear filled my veins. I suddenly realised what had been missing in the room the whole time: noise. I hadn't heard the heartbeat when they were scanning my stomach. Ben and Rhyz were non-plussed and didn't seem to understand what I had straightaway figured out. I turned to look at Ben, and he was smiling until he caught sight of my face, and then I tried to explain without causing alarm to Rhyz what was going on. I don't think he understood and I felt almost unable to move under the weight of what was going to happen next.

Tears filled my eyes as I realised what was happening, and as the doctors made the calls to the next hospital, I tried to hold it together enough not to let Rhyz see the terror in my face. We arrived at the specialist hospital, and a sonographer was waiting for us at the entry desk.

I somehow knew deep down what they were going to tell me, and I knew this wasn't going to be suitable for a young boy to watch or hear. I explained to Rhyz that I expected there was going to be some bad news ahead and l told him it was better if he stayed out of the room and that we wouldn't be too long. Poor, confused Rhyz sat next to the lovely elderly lady at the reception desk as we were hurried into an adjoining room.

The senior sonographer checked over my stomach again with the doppler, and then it was decided to do an internal ultrasound. A young lady was called into the room after they explained it was a legal requirement to have someone else present if an internal examination was going to be done. I just stared straight ahead at the monitor almost unable to blink, blocking everyone out. The sonographer began the examination, and I grimaced in pain and humiliation, willing myself not to cry as I held tight to Ben's hand.

After a few moments, the specialist turned and looked at me and said he was very sorry for our loss, but it looked as though our baby had died only a week or two earlier. I could barely comprehend the words coming out his mouth, and with tears rolling down my face, I blurted out, 'Take that ultrasound device out of me!'

I am not sure what protocol there is to follow when you tell someone that they have lost a baby. But lying there with my legs apart praying they could find a heartbeat and then being told there was none with the internal ultrasound device still inserted inside me was so degrading and made me feel more vulnerable than ever.

He apologised profusely, and I am sure he didn't mean any ill intent, but to me, it just felt like fate had served up karma in the cruellest way it possibly could. For all those wrongs I had done in my life: the abortion, leaving a marriage, being a stubborn teenager—this was my karma. I had brought it all on myself, and nothing could make me think otherwise.

I was inconsolable and felt so empty. I had taken away everyone's joy, and my body had betrayed me in the worst possible way. I hated myself with every fibre of my being. I felt as though I had let everyone I loved the most down, and I was getting my comeuppance.

I was left to get dressed and pull myself together before collecting Rhyz on the way out and explaining that we had lost the baby. The sadness in his eyes was heartbreaking and his little arms wrapped around me. 'I am so sorry, Mum,' he whimpered, and I held him close and said, 'Me too.'

Ben was still trying to comprehend what had just happened, and slow, fat tears rolled down his face as he tried to comfort us on the way back to the car. To add insult to injury, the hospital said they would need to do a 'D and C' (dilation and curettage, which is where they clean out your uterus) as my body was not naturally letting me miscarry. Unfortunately, they weren't able to do the procedure until the following week.

The thought of walking around with my baby inside me was too much to bear. It felt like a cruel reminder of my failures as a woman. I was distraught, and a decision was made by one of the doctors to prescribe me Valium® to help me cope. In this medically sedated state, the decision was made to attend an abortion clinic so that I would be able to have the D and C done within days instead.

I wept as I pushed past the picketers holding their anti-abortion placards high at the front entrance of the clinic. They didn't yell or talk to me but instead held their signs aloft with the words 'abortion is murder' and so forth as they stood on the edge of the curb. In my haze of tears and heartache, I yelled at them, 'Why don't you go and do something good instead of making people feel so horrible?'

Ben had to pull me away as I sobbed a list of places their presence would be more helpful, I am pretty sure the words 'serving food to the homeless' and such were used. Instead of retaliating, I remember their faces just looked sad, not for what I was saying but because of my sadness. They responded to the emotional and devastated young lady who had come to have her unborn baby surgically removed with words that, from memory, were kind and apologetic regarding my situation.

As the doctor did the compulsory ultrasound before the procedure, I asked her to double-check if there was a heartbeat. She looked at me strangely for a moment before realising why I was there and held my hand as she confirmed that I had, indeed, lost my baby.

I was beyond heartbroken.

CHAPTER 8

LIVING ON A PRAYER

Ben, Rhyz, and I spent the following weeks trying to put ourselves back together and recover from the grief that we felt. We decided to throw ourselves into wedding plans, which was a wonderful distraction during such a sad time. I left my second job at Rosie's so I could heal both emotionally and physically, and I comforted myself the best I could with the love and support of my family.

The feeling that I had caused it all never went away, and I vowed I would do anything in my power to give my fiancé and son the complete family we all so badly wanted and they so much deserved. I felt like I didn't deserve any further happiness; I'd had my share. All I wanted to do was make it right by having another baby.

We decided we would wait until after our wedding to start trying again. I went straight back on the pill as we picked out suits and a wedding dress and designed invitations and cakes. It was a comfort to know Ben would even still want me after I had lost our child. He didn't leave me or blame my body for failing to see the pregnancy through—instead, he brought me cups of tea in bed, and as a family we watched late-night movies when I couldn't sleep, eating lollies and being close.

He kept me going until I felt my hormones and body finally return to normal. Then, one day about three months before the wedding, I woke up with a terrible stomach bug. It lasted for days, and sure enough, even though I was taking the contraceptive pill again, that upset tummy was announcing I was once again expecting.

This time we were more cautious and scared to announce it or celebrate. We waited until the twelve-week scan and then allowed ourselves to believe it a little more. I had never been so happy to have morning sickness. Just as I was with Rhyz, my health suffered terribly, but this time there was comfort in the illness. It allowed me to know each day my baby was growing and still with me. I was around twenty weeks pregnant when we held a beautiful wedding in our backyard with our family and friends. Rhyz stood beside us and cried with happiness. It was a magical day, and we were thrilled to be starting our married life with our baby already healthily growing.

I began to struggle emotionally with the pregnancy. At first, I put it down to hormones being haywire after such a recent loss and the fact I was still vomiting around the clock. Then I had terrible migraines added to the mix. I attended my sixteen-week antenatal check-up at the hospital and in the privacy of the midwife's office. I broke down sobbing, explaining how terrible I felt. I still hadn't felt my baby move, and I just had this feeling something terrible was going to happen to the baby or me.

The midwife I saw was so kind and understanding and explained how common this was after having a traumatic first pregnancy and labour and then a recent miscarriage. She organised for me to get another ultrasound to settle my nerves and to return the following week to check in on my health.

The ultrasound was perfect, and the little heartbeat was strong and safe, although I couldn't feel it. I was reassured, and I could see on the screen that yes indeed, our baby was a very energetic little bunny. I returned as requested the following week and spoke again to the midwife and the doctors who had looked over the ultrasound, and they both assured me that all was well. They suggested that if I was struggling, perhaps talking to a psychiatrist might help. I told them I wouldn't need that and I would be fine. *Surely the hormones were playing havoc, and I would be less emotional soon,* I thought. This wasn't the case, and the final straw was when Ben came home from work to find me fully clothed, sobbing in the shower, insisting that something was wrong with our baby and I must be going crazy because I still couldn't feel it moving.

Ben made me call the doctor, and I agreed to attend weekly psychiatric sessions to assist me through what they were guessing was either PTSD or perinatal depression. I had to ask my boss to leave work early each Wednesday to attend these appointments, and they were very supportive. However, I couldn't get my head around it; no matter what we spoke about, it didn't change the fact that I kept insisting something was wrong.

I must have sounded like those people who go around wearing tinfoil hats and telling people the world was ending. But it didn't matter what evidence they put in front of me; I just kept deteriorating. I was only able to manage a few small bites of any meal and would immediately be horrendously sick, yet I had gained so much weight that I was being told to watch what sort of foods I was consuming for fear the calorie content was too high. I went above and beyond during this pregnancy to look after my health in every way possible. I made organic homemade chicken nuggets, but could only manage one or two before it all came back up again, and I continued to get bigger by the day.

We decided to get a 3D scan to find out the sex of the baby and the sonographer announced it was a boy and we all cheered. It made the pregnancy feel so much more real. The sonographer said there seemed to be a bit of extra amniotic fluid around the baby and to mention that at my next appointment with my doctors, which I did.

The pregnancy was taking its toll on me, and the psychiatrist had diagnosed a severe case of depression and PTSD and the reason I likely couldn't feel my baby kick is because I was such a driven career woman that my mind wouldn't allow me to feel it.

She would go further to elaborate that I had such a tough time during the last pregnancy with my turbulent relationship with Nick, that I was hanging on to the stability of my career as a safety net, and the thought of upsetting my work with a baby was causing me to not allow my mind to accept that I was pregnant.

I thought this sounded absolutely absurd and continued to insist that I actually couldn't feel any flutterings of my baby's movements and that I didn't have a fear of losing my career at all. Yet she persisted that it was exactly how she explained and continued to treat me for PTSD. It was suggested that maybe antidepressants would assist me during the next couple of months to help stabilise my mood and the dark reoccurring thoughts I was having about my unborn son or myself dying during labour.

I flatly refused to take any medication, but I never missed an appointment with her or the midwives. These doctor's visits were happening more regularly as I was just so unwell.

I remember fainting in the middle of a video store and struggling to walk more than a few metres at a time. As I approached thirty weeks, my body was so swollen that I constantly ached all over. I would wake up in tears from the pain. It was decided that due to the condition I was in, a caesarean section would be the safest option for everyone involved and I was sent for further scans to check growth and dates so we could book in for the birth.

Bubba, while looking like he was practising a jig inside me during every scan, was hardly cooperative, and one scan failed to find his bladder. 'He must have just emptied it,' they said. So I was to drink another couple of glasses of water and waddle around a bit and then go back in for them to capture it again. Yet he still refused to play the game, and as I was a heavily pregnant woman about to burst, they rescheduled for me to come back the following week. I must have had countless ultrasounds towards the end, as my tiny man was too busy swimming to play the game.

The doctor caring for me had decided to bring forward the caesarean to be done on my thirty-sixth week due to my sheer size.

After measuring my gigantic tummy and feeling his size and position, he declared that my son looked like he would be a good ten-pounder with a full head of hair; how he came to the hair conclusion just through feeling my stomach alone, I shall never know. I swear, I was secretly thankful that he was not going to be a vaginal birth after that comment.

I was sent a referral to yet another ultrasound specialist to be done the week before my booking to check we were good to go, and I was so excited that I was nearing the end of this seemingly never-ending pregnancy. One morning, the pain was excruciating throughout my body, not like contractions or anything remotely similar, just this feeling of pressure from every pore in my skin; my head was pounding as usual, and I was still terribly nauseous.

Ben insisted we head down to the hospital, at the very least for some form of pain relief. I didn't take much convincing, and we headed down with my pregnancy medical file, and I waddled into the maternity suite as instructed. A nurse coming my way showed us into the birthing suite, and I had to keep trying to explain I wasn't in labour; it was my body that hurt. I had been through this before and knew what a contraction felt like: this was certainly not it. She said it was okay and laughed like I was an amateur and ushered me on to the bed anyway. What happened next remains a bit of a blur, but they at some point realised that I was only thirty-five weeks pregnant and that signs were pointing to me being in labour after all. They said as I was not full term, they would be quickly organising me to be transferred to Perth's King Edward Hospital, which specialises in early labours and has all the specialists that my son and I might need.

I can remember them organising an ambulance, and I was to wait in the room. While this occurred, I was a little blasé as I knew I wasn't having contractions and I killed time by stepping on to the scales which showed me at 76 kg, a big jump from the 52 kg I was when I found out I was pregnant. I was put on a stretcher, which I kept insisting was unnecessary as I could waddle. 'I'm not in labour. This is all a little over the top.' As they put me into the ambulance to transfer me, I clearly remember someone reaching in and asking for my medical files that had been updated at every single appointment. Once they were retrieved, the doors were closed, and I was whisked away to King Edward Hospital, with Ben following in his car behind us.

I was taken in the emergency doors, and instantly I hopped off the stretcher and sat down on one of the chairs while the doctors were going over my file. I felt rather silly. *This is all very dramatic.* I wondered if I could just get a couple of paracetamol tablets and return home to rest. A senior midwife was walking past when she stopped a short way from me and stared me up and down, and then came over quite quickly, saying that she wanted me to come with her.

I was placed in a wheelchair and taken downstairs to an ultrasound room that had been shut down for the evening. The midwife turned on the lights and started to set up machines and kept asking me various questions that made the hairs on my neck stand up.

She wanted to know if I could feel the baby move, if I had migraines, what the other ultrasounds showed and each answer I gave her seemed to make her move faster, and her face grew sterner by the passing minute. She had a walkie-talkie with her that she turned on. Another nurse who had come down with us started to set up a sterile trolley beside the ultrasound machine.

It was as though they were about five steps in front of what I knew to be happening. The midwife ran the doppler over my stomach. The nurse who was standing close behind her leaned over her shoulder and took a sharp intake of breath.

By now, my thoughts were racing. *I can hear the heartbeat, what is all this fuss about? I still haven't had a contraction yet, so why is this so serious all of a sudden?* The midwife turned to me and started to explain I was in trouble. My baby had a rare condition called tracheoesophageal fistula (TOF), and there were a few other things she could see that might be of concern.[3] Right now, though, they needed to start draining my stomach of the vast amounts of amniotic fluid that had built up. She tried to explain that my son's oesophagus wasn't attached to his stomach—there was a gap, which meant he was not swallowing the fluid in utero like he should have been and instead I was swollen with it.

I tried to take it in what she said. It seemed simple enough. She said it would be okay and they can easily do surgery on him when he is born to repair it. But for now, we needed to start getting the fluid under control.

She went on to tell me that I couldn't have possibly felt my tiny baby kick as he was swimming in such a large amount of fluid.

'But my baby is almost ten pounds,' I insisted, 'My caesarean has been moved forward because he is so big.' She shook her head and said she wasn't sure how to tell me this, but he looked more around the mid-three-pound mark.

I was starting to panic; the other nurse was setting up the trolley with syringes, and they were going to start drawing the amniotic fluid out directly from my stomach. I was still trying to take this all in when the midwife said she was just going to do a quick internal check to make sure I wasn't having contractions. The very moment she started to do the exam my waters broke everywhere. I started screaming, and while she was telling the nurse to make a call, I was pleading. 'I need to have caesarean, I can't have a natural labour, I will die, and this is all a big mistake!'

This lady—I wish I knew her name—clearly had me sized up in a heartbeat and knew I was just petrified but was not going to calm down. She leaned in, grabbing me by my shoulders, and told me in no uncertain terms to pull myself together. She looked me directly in the eyes and sternly told me, 'If you don't give birth naturally, your son, who looks like he is very unwell, is going to die.'

It worked, and I stopped screaming. I was now absolutely frozen with fear. Her strong words were what I needed to snap back to reality and keep from losing my grip.

They managed to get me off the table, with my waters still pouring out, and put me in a wheelchair. I think the seriousness of it all kicked in when they started running with me down the hall.

The nurse was communicating with other staff on what I assume to be a walkie-talkie, and the midwife pushing my wheelchair, as she ran through corridors. A code started blaring over the speakers, for me. They were calling for another ambulance and more doctors to come from Princess Margaret Hospital and talking about a quick transfer for my son the moment he was born.

Every single fear I'd had in the past few months was becoming a reality, and now I had doctors and nurses running in every direction setting up to try to save my son's life. I hadn't been going crazy at all, and it wasn't PTSD: my son was sick, and now we were about to try to keep him alive.

When the nurse rounded the corner into a large birthing suite, there were at least eight people in the room. The nurses helped me stand from the wheelchair; my eyes opened wide with fear as this huge avalanche of amniotic fluid continued to rush out of me, drenching the floor and making a couple of nurses rush for towels in the adjoining bathroom.

There was so much commotion that it was hard to comprehend what was happening. I was terrified. The hospital staff stripped me naked within seconds and wrapped a hospital gown on me as they attached morphine allergy tags to my wrist. There were now doctors entering the room and talking quickly amongst themselves as I was lifted into the hospital bed by the gentle midwives.

As I moved onto the bed, I looked down to see that my enormous bump had disappeared, leaving an empty stomach of loose skin behind, and I gasped in fear. A nurse who had taken it to be her job to sit right by my side and hold my hand explained that it was okay, it was all the amniotic fluid I had lost, but now they had to move quickly to get my son out before he possibly turned the wrong way and made the delivery more difficult. There were people everywhere; cannulas were being placed in my arms to get ready for the drips that were being hung on the IV stands by more nurses.

I was given an epidural as they were about to start pumping my body full of synthetic drugs that would speed up my contractions, which I had yet to feel. Ben, who had been by my side the entire time, stood in absolute terror at the side of my bed as the commotion bustled around me at such a fast but well-coordinated pace. They had the neonatal baby resuscitation unit ready on one side of my bed, and everything seemed to happen so fast it was hard to take it all in. I had every monitor possible attached to my body, and they emphasised we were running out of time to get my son out.

The doctors never left the room and stood at the back, talking on the phones to the incoming hospital team organising what was about to happen next. They kept reassuring me that at thirty-five weeks, a baby's lungs are pretty good and he may be able to even breathe on his own, but they would need to take him to the specialised neonatal unit the moment he was born.

The nurse who sat beside me throughout just kept talking nonstop to distract me. She was kind and sweet, and I truly felt that I had my best friend in the room with me.

I was given gas, more likely than not to keep me calm, and I was only alerted to contractions when the nurse read the monitor to the doctors, who were constantly telling them to speed it up. The doors burst open with a flurry, and an entirely new team of doctors arrived with a different type of transport baby crib and joined the others in the back of the room while the nurses held my hand, stroked my hair, and reassured me I was in the best hands possible.

His heartbeat was lost quite a few times due to his size and the large area he was now able to move in, at one stage they physically pushed on my wobbly empty skin of a stomach and seemingly manoeuvred him down into place. With the help of attachments on his head to monitor his heart rate, they made the contractions speed up once again. With the use of vacuum extraction, they pulled his tiny little body quietly from mine. Every person in the room seemed to be holding their breath, and then the sound that I so desperately needed to hear emerged from this fragile little soul, and he let out a soft cry.

You instantly felt the room take in a collective breath. That moment of pause, of utter celebration, was pure joy. *We did it!* The very next moment, the race was on once more. In a beautiful gesture, a quick-thinking nurse grabbed Ben's phone from him and started taking photos. The doctors had swarmed forward the moment he had emerged, and the warm, brightly-lit transport cubicle stood waiting beside my bed.

They wrapped my son in a blanket, and the doctor put him in my arms for a fleeting moment without even taking their hands off him. I was able to look at this beautiful, but incredibly small and fragile-looking soul before he was whisked away and into Ben's arms. Ben softened as he also felt his baby's warmth before the medical team placed our son into the waiting crib and sprinted out of the door.

Our son was born less than two hours from when we landed in the emergency room of this incredible hospital that undoubtedly had just saved his life. Ben stood frozen, and I remember telling him to go with our son. He ran through the doors after our little boy as he was spirited away down the corridor. Then, the doctors turned to me: I had started to haemorrhage and was struggling immensely.

They reacted fast, managing to quickly treat and stem the bleeding and apply the oxygen I needed. These beautiful nurses and midwives were amazing. They distracted me, comforted me, and kept me up to date with what was happening. Even in my groggy state, I was so grateful they were there for me. Doctors kept coming in to check I was stabilising and letting me know that our son was still fighting and was getting the treatment he needed and assured me they would keep me up to date. The nurses organised cups of tea and toast for me while we waited for the epidural to wear off, and had an upbeat chat about the various baby names we had thought of for our son. Ben and I hadn't finalised our decision, but when he returned after accompanying our son as far as he was allowed to go, we decided that we would call him Corbin Beau.

The nurses helped me into a wheelchair, and as I was so weak from haemorrhaging, I was unable to move properly, so they gently wheeled me into the bathroom and washed my hair and my body and dressed me in a fresh gown. They then brushed my hair and helped to feed me the toast and tea that was organised earlier, as I was still so shaky and drained from what had just happened. I really can't praise them enough. I look back now and know that everyone in the room was preparing for the worst. Their professionalism and the way they treated me with such respect throughout has always remained in my mind.

When I was stable enough to be moved out of the suite, they wheeled me into a room to settle in for some rest; I wasn't placed on the maternity ward. I am not sure if this is common for mothers who have not been able to take their babies back with them, but it was a thoughtful gesture that I appreciated. I am not sure I would have coped very well being among new babies while mine was not able to be by my side. The doctors came in and let me know that Corbin would be undergoing surgery at Princess Margaret Hospital at 9 am the next morning. I think it was about midnight at that stage. To stabilise him, they kept him in the neonatal intensive care unit (NICU) as he was not quite up to being transferred at the time. They said I wasn't able to see him straight away but promised me I could go down the following morning before he left and visit him.

Even with all the drugs in my system, I barely slept a wink for fear of missing my chance to see my son before he left. I was wide awake by 6 am. Due to protocol and my weakness, I was still confined to a wheelchair. I was able to be wheeled down to the NICU and see my son for the first time. He looked so peaceful and was sleeping, but was covered in tubes and monitoring devices. It was then that it was explained he had been placed in an induced coma and was on life support so his little body didn't have to work so hard to breathe for itself.

The driver of the ambulance who was transporting him to Princess Margaret Hospital waited patiently as we took photos and touched his soft skin and whispered how much we loved him. It was time to prep him for transfer, and we were asked to leave the NICU and go back to the room. I made Ben go past the gift shop on the way back, and I bought a stuffed otter toy that I clung to and planned to give to Corbin when we arrived at his bedside at the new hospital. I held that tiny otter close to my stomach and wept as I ached for my son to be in its place.

I managed to eat breakfast on the doctors' orders, changed into clean clothes, and waited for permission to be discharged so that I could be there for Corbin when he came out of surgery. As I was changing in the bathroom, I noticed a set of scales and, fully clothed within nine hours of giving birth, I stepped on them. Remembering that I weighed in at 76 kg just before I had gone into labour, I watched as 64 kg showed up in front of me. Taking into consideration that Corbin only weighed 1.8 kg and the average weight of a placenta is 500 g, that leaves almost 10 kg worth of amniotic fluid.

No wonder I was in pain. My stomach was instantly flat. Loose skin was still there, but to look at me, it appeared I was never pregnant at all. It is the strangest feeling to put into words, but when I woke up that morning, all the pain had gone from my body. The pressure in my skin, my headaches, nausea, all gone. My emotional state was relieved, which sounds so terrible because of the situation, but it was as though the moment Corbin was born that constant feeling of depression and dread had lifted. I felt clear-minded for the first time in months.

Of course, I was hugely emotional and beside myself with fear for what would happen next, but not in that terrible way where I had started to believe I was going crazy. I had believed the specialists when they said my mind didn't want me to feel my baby move, which is the most horrible thing to be told. I begged the doctors for a fast discharge, and with the promise to get check-ups at the next hospital's NICU, I was allowed to leave before lunchtime.

I had no idea what to expect when I walked through the doors of the NICU for the first time, but I don't think anything can prepare you for it. It had double-secured airlocked doors with the reception desk in the middle that gave you access onto the main floor, where the most heartbreaking and heartwarming scenes take place. If you have not had to enter through such doors, then those two contradicting words would not make much sense. But to those who have called it home, it is self-explanatory.

For those who have not experienced a NICU ward, let me tell you a little about Ward 6B, which is the neonatal intensive care ward where every sick baby from around Western Australia comes for care. It's a place where any parent would trade their soul for the possibility of being able to one day walk out of those doors with their child. It is where brand new parents come, ashen-faced, their hearts in their throats as they pray for a miracle for their long-awaited child. Parents rush in daily, often straight from the birthing suite, to comfort their new baby who, like mine, was whisked away at birth amid chaos and panic.

Not knowing what to expect, the usual reaction is a flood of tears and racking sobs from the parents as they see their baby hooked up to sterile, complex machines, covered in tubes, IVs and monitors. In 6B, you watch hearts break, dreams shatter, and lives changed in an instant. If you are lucky, you witness a miracle. Even if it is not your miracle, the rush of overwhelming emotions still affects you as though it was. It means the next miracle could be yours. It is that hope that keeps your spirits up, and it's the faith—sometimes blind—that keeps you believing in the doctors' competence.

But it's a fact that every night when you go home, you leave your heart behind you with your child on the ward. Some nights, following a traumatic day, a bedside vigil is often kept.

Soft voices of weary mothers whispering lullabies to their babies echo through the darkened ward. Fathers' voices cracking as they tell their child the dreams and hopes for their future break through the sound of beeping monitors and bubbling breathing machines. Quiet sobs and hugs are often shared between parents who together understand the pain, torment, and the heartache of the whole situation. The words 'it's not fair' and 'I don't understand why' are replayed like a broken record, bouncing off the walls by each parent who enters. Ward 6B is entirely its own world. Once you enter those doors, the world outside fades away and seems trivial and materialistic.

The worry of whether your pram has a multitude of functions and can hold a coffee cup pales in comparison to the world you are now thrust into. Pleading, begging, bargaining to God, spirits, or whatever higher belief you have are common rituals there. The unfairness of it all doesn't make sense most days. The babies in here have been greatly anticipated new additions to the family. Some couples may have waited years to conceive, suffering miscarriages, stillbirths, and resorting to IVF. Most of these mothers watched their pregnancy diligently, taking care of their health, exercising, eating well, taking the advised multivitamins, and avoiding the long list of banned pregnancy foods and drinks. They would have gone to every doctors' appointment, followed all the guidelines, and still, their baby ended up there. No-one in 6B did anything to warrant being there.

Every single mother and father will, at some stage, ask themselves what they did wrong during the pregnancy, before becoming pregnant, or even in a past life, to try to understand the suffering they are going through now. The truth is, nothing could have prevented their baby's journey to 6B, and it reinforces the message that sometimes in life, bad things really do happen to good people. And now it was happening to me.

1999. The yellow caravan in the foreground was my home. I was 15 years old.

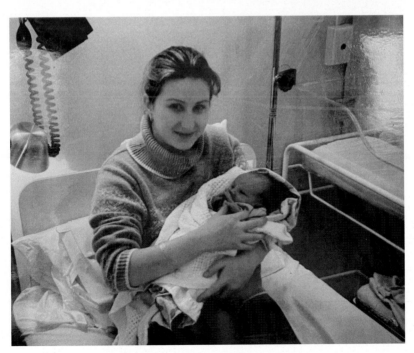

2000. The day my son Rhyz was born.

Rhyz first day of grade 1.

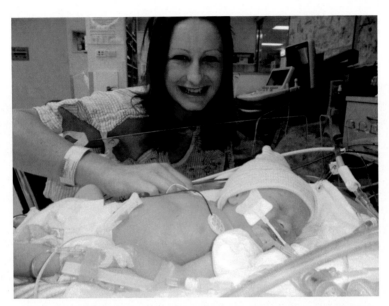

A few hours after Corbin was born. He was on life support in the NICU at King Edward Hospital. This was moments prior to being transferred to Princess Margaret Hospital for his first operation.

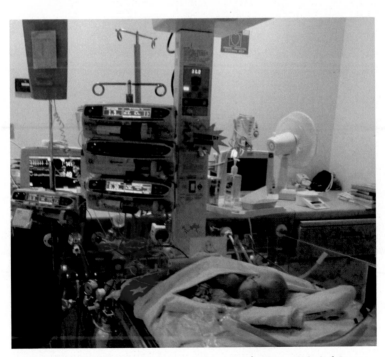

Corbins isolation ward in Princess Margaret Hospital, NICU 6B.

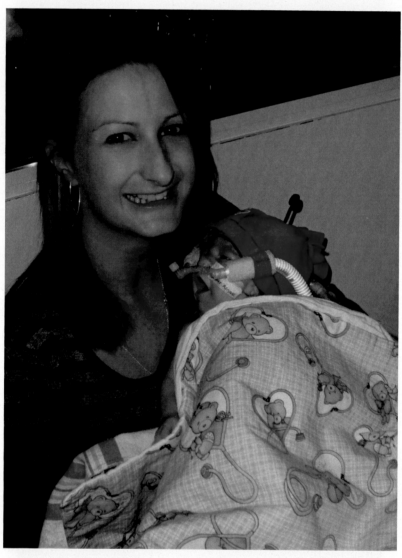

A brief snuggle moment in the NICU when Corbin was off life support and on CPAP breathing device.

Mothers Day surprise, the first time we left the NICU ward. Rhyz is holding the oxygen sensor and we were accompanied by a senior nurse for our 30 minutes together in fresh air.

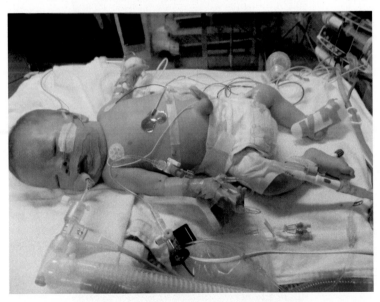

The day following mothers day Corbin had his riskiest and longest surgery to date, his 8 hour Kasai procedure. He was placed back on life support to recover.

With Rhylz in his final year at high school and Corbin just beginning school, we certainly had a busy household.

Luke and I arriving elated at our "engagement party" after eloping days earlier.

Photo courtesy of Simon Malfitana from Street Angles

Rhylz after marching out from the school of infantry.
My family. My world.

Having a successful business has allowed me to use my social platform to be able to make a positive difference in the community. My charity, Driven by KM is certainly my proudest career achievement to date. My husband Luke is my best friend and the love of my life. I am so grateful that we get to experience this wonderful life together.

Photo courtesy of Simon Malfitana from Street Angles.

Photo courtesy of Simon Malfitana from Street Angles.

CHAPTER 9

THE FEAR

When I arrived at Princess Margaret Hospital, I steadied myself for what may happen. Next, I was wheeled into the room in my wheelchair (the haemorrhaging had weakened me considerably, making it hard to hold myself upright, let alone walk) past the glass sealed doors, and into a world that I hadn't seen before but would sadly soon call my second home.

With my throat tight the whole way, I tried to take in as much of the surroundings as possible. I was thoroughly out of my depth in my ability to comprehend what all the noises and machines and hustling of important people in scrubs meant. A nurse called Shannon introduced herself as we made our way through to the main floor, and she ushered us towards an infant-sized resuscitation bed that was set up in the far left-hand corner of the ward. As I got closer, the overwhelming array of tubes and pumps that were connected to Corbin came into view, and I felt myself almost leave my body with the rush of emotion that poured through me. I pushed myself out of the wheelchair and hobbled as fast as I could to see my son.

The overwhelming urge to be as close as possible came over me through the searing pain my own body was feeling. I remember a tall bedside chair placed right next to him where the nurse had been sitting only moments earlier, monitoring our son. In an attempt to see my small, vulnerable bundle I tried to gently move it to the side, not realising that it had rubber grips on the base to make it stable, and all I managed to do was topple it to the floor in my haste. By now Shannon had caught up with me and was trying to comfort me as I attempted to bend down and replace the chair, and all the while my shallow, short breaths belied my ability to hide my fear.

There he was, naked under lights, attached to humming machines, with so many tubes that I didn't understand the meaning of, although I certainly knew they were keeping him alive. My hand instinctively reached out to touch him and then hovered mid-air as I didn't know what I could touch. Each little part was delicately frail and had medication lines emerging from or dressed in surgical tape. My face crumpled as I turned back to Ben who was standing in shock at the foot of the bed, and I gripped tightly to the side of his bed as I felt my knees buckle underneath me as my heart shredded into pieces and drained my last ray of hope from me.

Shannon gently touched my shoulder and explained that we needed to go and sterilise our hands together, and she would talk me through what was happening. She helped me get back into the wheelchair and calmly explained how our new world would look. Shannon said it in such a matter-of-fact way that the tears stopped and I was able to start processing what was happening around me. She explained we weren't going to be able to hold him for a while until he stabilised, and that in these circumstances there aren't timelines set as each little body is different and we would have to learn to follow his lead. Her confidence soothed my initial panic, and we made our way back to my baby after sterilising ourselves.

I was reintroduced to my son, who was fresh from his successful TOF repair surgery, and I was now able to notice the nurses buzzing around his bed where he lay. He had a drain coming from the side of his lungs at the back, a nasogastric feeding tube was taped to his face and ran through his nose, multiple IVs pumped various pain medications and antibiotics into the veins found in his limbs. His tiny, swollen body was once again relying on a machine to breathe life into his little lungs, and the lack of noise or movement he made due to the sedation made me feel like this whole situation was surreal.

The specialists assured me everything had gone to plan and I recall asking someone how long he would take to recover from this. I was told ten days was the usual recovery time from this surgery.

They then mentioned some abnormalities had shown up and he would need to go back into the theatre the following day. His anus was not perforated, and they weren't sure if his intestines and bowel were sitting in the correct places. So, the first step was going to be creating a stoma and adding a colostomy bag so he could expel faeces before they stabilised him to do further surgery on his anus and join his bowel to where it needed to be.

They said that while the TOF repair was successful, he did show signs of oesophageal atresia, which meant basically that his throat or windpipe was floppy and would collapse on itself, rendering him unable to breathe in his current state. They mentioned he had three kidneys which, while not causing any concerns at the time, did indicate he might well have a rare condition called VACTERL association.[4] VACTERL is an acronym that stands for the following:

V: Vertebral anomalies

A: Anal atresia (imperforated anus)

C: Cardiac issues (Atrial septal defects)

T: Tracheoesophageal fistula

E: Esophageal atresia ('floppy trachea' is what I call this one)

R: Renal anomalies and / or radial anomalies (the three kidneys and hypospadias)

L: Limb deformities (we didn't have any signs of this at all)

They warned me not to search for it on the internet, and I didn't. I was too scared about what I might find. The doctors started to go through the list of what surgeries he would need to repair these issues and at what stage in life these would occur.

I realised that maybe we wouldn't be going home in a week or two, and prepared myself for slowly working through the list of follow-up procedures and tests and started to get into a routine that would make it bearable. The surgery to add a stoma to Corbin went without a hitch, and after a week in the hospital, I was able to hold my baby.

Shannon once again was there and sat me down in a giant plastic chair next to Corbin's care station. Another nurse helped to hold up the attached tubing and drainage so as not to entangle it. Shannon carefully lifted his tiny body off the bed for the first time and placed him against my chest. With my arms gingerly wrapped around him, I hoped I was not causing him any pain, but at the same time, I wanted his little soul to be as close to my heart as I could possibly get him.

Tears rolled down my face, and my heart swelled from the happiness and hope that this simple action gave me. You could not wipe the smile off my face, and a shakily recorded video taken by Ben shows my whole face light up in a way that illuminates the whole room. For the few moments I had with him in my arms, I knew it was going to be okay; we were going to keep fighting together, and he would one day forever be in my arms.

He still had IVs attached to cannulas on every limb, but the doctors assured me he was a fighter and was holding on strong. He was slightly jaundiced, but due to him being a little early that was to be expected, and along with all the different machines, he was given a tiny soft baby eye mask and bathed in bright lights while he started to gain his strength back.

There is no answer as to why not one of these very prominent and apparent medical conditions remained unseen on the multiple ultrasounds, or why the polyhydramnios (the extreme excess fluid I was carrying) wasn't diagnosed during my pregnancy. I decided early on never to ask. I learnt I had a minimal amount of energy, and I was putting every remaining ounce I had left into focusing on getting through the days and remaining positive. I had—and still have—no interest in looking at the negatives or being buried down in things that were not going to change the current situation.

I have often wondered if it was protocol for my pregnancy medical file to be taken off me as they transferred me from the hospital that had been overseeing my health to King Edward Hospital. It contained notes about all of my appointments, test results, and psych visits. I never heard from my doctor or that hospital again, but I did get a phone call within forty-eight hours of giving birth to Corbin from the psychiatrist who I had seen weekly over the previous four months. I was waiting to get into an elevator at the hospital as I took the call, and she told me she had heard I had given birth to my son. I know that she'd had to rely on the records the doctors had passed on saying that my baby and I were completely healthy, but I had spent the months prior being told by this woman I that was imagining all my symptoms, I didn't want to feel my baby, and my mind was making me wrongly believe what resulted in being true.

'Oh, Ang, I heard that you had your son and that you are in hospital, I hope that you are coping okay and that he is getting better,' she sympathetically said into my ear. I was well aware that I had people within earshot, but I didn't have anything left to hide, and I was in no way going to sugar-coat something that had been served to me rather bitterly over the previous months as something that was all in my head.

So I took a deep breath. 'Yes, you are right; my son is sick, just as I feared he was and had tried to convince you. He will be spending a long time in NICU and undergoing surgeries and is currently on life support.' I heard her breath draw in, and she tried to say 'Oh, I am sorry,' but I kept talking right over the top of her. 'So, I ask that you and everyone else surrounding you who insisted this was all in my head throughout my pregnancy do not ever contact me again.' And I hung up on her.

I no longer had time for any negativity, and even if apologies were coming my way, it wasn't going to help my son now. I chose to move on and let it be a lesson that sometimes your intuition is screaming at you to pay attention and that even professionals get it wrong sometimes.

*

We lived almost fifty minutes away from the hospital, and Ben decided that it would be better for him to continue to work and save his holidays for a time in the future when he may urgently need to take them. I understood, but it started to cause a lot of pressure on us as a couple as I struggled to keep it all going alone.

Rhyz, who was not a parent and therefore not allowed on the ward at all, had only seen his brother in photos we would take and bring home to show him. It was a horrible period while we adjusted to our new reality. Rhyz was emotionally devastated and, like the rest of us, absolutely unsettled by the curveball we had just been thrown. He asked about his brother every moment, and his little heart was just as shattered as the rest of ours.

Just when you think life can't keep kicking you down any further, a rapid succession of shit landed at our feet.

Within weeks of Corbin's birth, the owner of the rental property sold our home, and we were given short notice to vacate. I was too exhausted to put up a fight by this stage, and we set about finding a new home while juggling the world around us. In between the hospital visits and caring for Rhyz, I started packing our house up by myself. Ben was working shifts, and all of this came out of the blue. During this time, the trauma of everything I was attempting to do physically caused me to haemorrhage again. I was taken back into hospital for treatment. I insisted on being released the same day as I had no-one else to pick up the pieces. I needed to be there for both my sons.

Corbin, who had started to be weaned off life support, was now using a CPAP (continuous positive airway pressure) system to assist his breathing as he recuperated. He contracted pneumonia and was ushered into an isolated room on the open ward for infection control and one-on-one care. This rollercoaster wouldn't slow down, and I didn't know how to emotionally comprehend the pain that struck deep each time a new complication arose. It was one foot in front of the other, and some days I don't even know how I did it. I do know the only thing that kept me going was my sons—both of them, every day without fail. They were the reason I got up every morning and faced it head-on, no matter how tough it got, and by God, did it get tougher.

Corbin's right lung collapsed, and he was placed back on life support as he was unable to breathe on his own. Infection after infection rolled through his body, and various concoctions of antibiotics were pumped through him to alleviate the problems. Once again, he was unable to be touched, and with steroids being added to his list of medications to help his failing lungs, his body swelled as it tried to cope with it all. His blood sugar kept doing strange things and dropping rapidly, but tests that could explain this came back clear, and it was dismissed when it showed signs of normalising.

I seriously felt that I was a human walking around missing part of myself during this period. *What had I done to make my son suffer this torment and how could I possibly make it okay?* The powerlessness of it all reminded me of all those years when I had no control over my life. I just knew I had to keep standing, no matter how many times the wind got knocked out of me.

Corbin's jaundice disappeared, and he started to react well to the medication regime and once again was taken off life support and placed back on the CPAP device. His lungs strengthened, and he fought off the pneumonia and stabilised enough to start to undergo his planned surgeries. The extreme swelling had caused two hernias, which were to be taken care of next. His poor little bottom still needed to be repaired down the track to make sure his bowel would work when they eventually reversed the stoma and took away the colostomy bag.

He was still in isolation as he was weak, but I was able within the first month to give him his first bath and could now hold him for short periods. I remained as upbeat and positive as I possibly could manage.

My daily regime attending to Rhyz and Corbin looked like this: wake up at 5 am and call the ward to see how Corbin had gone overnight, then drive fifty minutes to the hospital and race in before doctors rounds to check on him. I would talk to the nurse overseeing him that day and spend thirty minutes to an hour gently wiping his face with a soft flannel if he was stable and stroking his hand and reading to him from the mountain of books I had placed in his room. I would then drive home in time to make breakfast, see Rhyz off to school, where I would then turn around and go back to the hospital in time to see the doctors on their daily rounds. I would spend my day watching my son undergo blood transfusions, surgical procedures, hourly blood tests, and a variety of other x-rays, ultrasounds, and exams until 2 pm. I would leave to collect Rhyz from school and settle down for dinner together before tucking him in for the night. Ben would then watch Rhyz as I headed back up to the hospital for the evening. I would spend another hour or two reading to Corbin in the dark and peaceful ward before heading home for the night to shower and settle into my PJs. After a final call to the hospital to check again on his progress around midnight, I would fall asleep, ready to do it all over again the next day.

Ben was still working, and his shifts would vary week to week, which made it hard for him to be there as often as I could be. But he was always there singing softly and holding Corbin at every chance he got. Ben started suffering from anxiety and panic attacks that made it harder for him to be there. Some days, he wasn't able to push past them, and I would face the day alone; it was hard on us both. Everyone deals with grief in their unique way. While he was there physically sometimes, emotionally, we were on different wavelengths as we coped in whatever way helped us get through. He threw himself into work, believing that providing for his family was the best place for him, as he did struggle to comprehend and understand the complexities of what was happening to our son. He was as heartbroken as I was, and although we went through it all together, it felt much more like a separate process.

Ben and I tried hard to keep positive for Rhyz at home. Rhyz had started to develop alopecia, and bald spots were appearing on his head due to the stress of this gut-wrenching turmoil he was going through. The brother he had been desperate for was fighting for his life daily instead of being home in his big brother's arms. It was sheer hell. He was starting to get bullied at school for his noticeable hair loss, and I don't know if that poor child had felt any more depressed than he did at the time. It was cruel and unfair, and my heart ached for him as it did for the rest of us.

Corbin's little veins were starting to play havoc, and they regularly collapsed, which was such a challenge to watch. They held down a tiny baby every other day and poked and prodded in all his limbs to find a new vein to keep the medications pumping. At this stage, he was still only able to take feeds via the nasogastric tube. A hopeless attempt to see if he could swallow had resulted in him aspirating the milk straight onto his lungs and set him back a million steps at once, causing a lung infection, so back onto the life support it was. It also confirmed the new diagnosis of having a laryngeal cleft, which causes food or fluid to pass into the airway, hence the aspiration issue.

Now and then his blood sugar kept throwing odd numbers for no reasons. The tests that were taken from the various organs would come back showing stable numbers. No-one knew what was causing this, but as with the jaundice, which would flare up and go away again, it wasn't our highest priority; it kept appearing to sort itself out. It was dismissed while the focus was put back onto the lungs that once again had another infection. Keeping him breathing was obviously the principal focus.

One day, Ben and I walked through the doors and the faces of everyone at reception when they saw us were pure white. We hadn't taken more than three steps into the ward when we realised the doctors were swarmed around Corbin. His windows, for the first time, had the curtains pulled down, and the parents in the open ward all stood as the monitors seemed to scream from our son's room. We rushed into his room to see the doctors resuscitating our son, and instantly, a nurse appeared and gently, but forcefully, led us out of the room and back into the reception corridor.

She tried to console us and explained they had been attempting to wean him off life support and go back on to the CPAP, but his body wasn't coping. They were going to do everything they could and would be placing him back on life support once they stabilised him. We were told to wait in the parents' lounge, and like ghosts, we stumbled over our feet as we made our way around the corner into the adjoining room. We sat rocking back and forth and feeling time standing still as we waited for someone to enter and tell us we could go back on the ward. Other parents came in, took one look at our faces and quickly disappeared, realising the severity of what was happening and giving us the space we needed.

It felt like an eternity. We sat and waited. I had never really believed in God, and I believed in him less when my son was born. But I ran to the bathroom and dropped to my knees and begged Him to save Corbin, that I would spend my life making it up to Him by being a good person and He could just take me instead, if only He spared my son. After what felt like an eternity, the doctors appeared and told us they had managed to get Corbin back on life support and he was semi-stable. We could come in and see him. I just closed my eyes tight as my heart started to beat again. Emotions this high have a way of almost numbing you as you move into an autopilot mode of coping; I guess it is so you can deal with it and not break into a million pieces.

Ben and I held each other's hands tightly and sobbed quietly in relief and fear as we made our way back onto the ward and into our sons' room, where doctors had gathered around his bed. He went back on the steroids and this time, due to the worrying blood sugars, was placed on another drug called diazoxide to try to prevent them dropping dangerously low. This time, however, Corbin didn't bounce back. In fact, it all started to go wrong very quickly. His oxygen levels kept dipping, his heart was showing signs of stress, and his blood tests began to indicate that his kidneys were reacting badly and his liver was acting strangely.

Ben's parents and family in Victoria had been incredibly supportive from day one. At least one family member was always with us during this time, and when Ben's dad, who Rhyz called 'Pop', came over, he decided he was going to introduce Rhyz to his brother come hell or high water. Now, Pop is a good, solid man, towering well over six feet tall, but, like his son, is an absolute softie with a heart of gold. One day when they all came up to the hospital, Pop grabbed Rhyz by the hand and marched straight through the glass doors and right past the reception desk and all the nurses and doctors and ushered Rhyz straight into Corbin's room. I don't know if it was because Corbin was in such a bad way that no-one stopped him, or maybe it was the look of determination across Pop's face and the sad look of a young boy who had desperately waited nearly three months to meet his brother. Not a single person whispered a word in our direction.

With Corbin now swollen from steroids, his eyes were squeezed shut with the pressure and his body unable to move. He was once again attached to every machine possible. I watched as Rhyz bent down to kiss his brother's forehead, and tears rolled down my face. I will be forever grateful for Pop doing that. We didn't know how much time we had left and he stepped up and gave Rhyz the chance to see who we were all fighting for.

Within days, Corbin's condition worsened, and when a nurse asked me to just gently lift Corbin so that we could place silicone-like gel pads under his body to prevent sore spots, I watched in horror as his eyes rolled back. His body instantly turned a shade of blue, deepening by the second. Once again, the doctors raced in and grabbed the lifeless body from my arms as I backed myself into the corner and watched as they started to resuscitate him and bring him back once again. I shook for the next hour. When all the machines had been reset and he was stable, I ran to the bathroom and threw up all over myself. We were moved onto the main floor after that, where the doctors could be within arm's reach. Before we left the isolation room, I remember getting the courage to ask the nurse on duty a question I had wanted to ask for the months prior: 'Is he going to be okay?' I choked these words out in a scared and cracking voice. *Please say yes, please don't hesitate, please just say yes and make it okay,* I thought desperately.

'I can't say that. I'm sorry, we don't know, and we aren't able to give you that news. I am sorry,' she said, looking sadly at my hunched shoulders and exhausted face. Although I already knew this was the response I would get, my heart broke all over again. No-one could work out what was going wrong. There were so many issues, and just when we thought we had one under control, it would circle back again. There were more tests, more ultrasounds, more specialists, and no answers. I had been keeping track of every blood test result and test in an exercise book, trying to keep up to date with what was happening. We were ruling things out but not making any ground. The only thing that went back to normal was his blood sugars, and they were able to take him off diazoxide. Within days, his various test results showed a massive improvement, coming back into the normal range.

His oxygen levels started to improve, and by day three of being on the main ward and off just one drug, he was able to be taken off life support and put back onto CPAP again. It was looking up. I kept telling myself, *It was just a blip. There were going to be ups and downs and the body would regulate itself and, of course, he would come out fighting.*

Sure enough, he came off CPAP and was back to breathing on his own and needed no steroids or antibiotics. We were moved back into the isolation ward; Corbin's little body was fragile, and his weak immune system couldn't risk catching anything else. We slowly started to see the light. He stabilised enough to get his anus repaired and thankfully that was so much simpler than expected and went perfectly. A couple more blood transfusions and he was perking up.

*

Corbin had a little iPod that was attached to tiny headphones, through which I softly played a mixture of Frank Sinatra and Jimmy Barnes to him during quiet periods on the ward. I spent every moment working my way through reading the entire collection of Enid Blyton's *The Faraway Tree* out loud to him and was now on to the Dr Suess books. Slowly, but surely, this smiling little fighter was coming on in leaps and bounds.

I had decorated his room as much as was allowed to make it feel more homely; I had pretty tiny crystals that hung from the IV stand, and soft-coloured muslin wraps laid across the chairs and at the end of his bed. There were family photos stuck near his bed and a pretty light that shone images on the ceiling to brighten the room softly. This was only allowed when he was stable and breathing on his own or not at risk of infection.

I had tried to bring as much happiness and normality into the bleak atmosphere as possible. We spent Easter in his isolated room, and a beautiful mother, Sammi, who I had become close to, spent days with me organising decorations for the rooms; buntings and bunny crafts to hang throughout the wards and chocolates for parents and nurses. You took every chance you got to bring joy and lift spirits because you knew just how taxing it was to the soul. Mothers would leave a packet of biscuits at your door or a cup of coffee, and some days that was all it took to keep you going. It was the biggest learning experience of my life to see how the smallest gesture can mean so much; it doesn't cost anything to be kind, and sometimes you never know how much it is appreciated by the person receiving that kindness.

Corbin started to get his less life-threatening surgeries ticked off. His stoma was reversed, and his colostomy bag removed. It went perfectly, and things were looking up. As long as there was a tiny bit of hope, that was all I needed to keep going. I lived by the mantra that my dad had said to me once: 'Take it day by day, hour by hour if you need to, and on the bad days—minute by minute.' Just keep going and focus on what the situation is at the time and keep the blinkers on to everything else. I use this saying still to this day, and it helps me keep things in perspective.

Then one day, a couple of weeks into his upturn, they checked Corbin's blood sugars, and they were sitting dangerously low, with absolutely no explanation and no signs at all. Not to worry—we would add the diazoxide to his now minimal medication regime and get them back into line. But that didn't happen quite as expected. Within forty-eight hours, we were back on the main floor and on life support with organs shutting down left, right, and centre. 'This was it,' I said, 'It's the diazoxide! It's shutting him down.'

I went through all the notes I had kept. The doctors kept insisting that it couldn't possibly be causing it; no-one had recorded an allergy, and it still didn't explain the blood sugars acting up in the first place. It didn't matter what made sense; I was filled with dread. I refused to leave and insisted they let me have an emergency bed in the next corridor. I sat at Corbin's bedside until 4 am when the nurse beside me told me to please go home and get some rest.

We had spent the past eight hours talking, and she agreed something was off and told me to be a lot more confident in expressing my concerns with the doctors in the morning.

Now, I know Corbin's care was incredible and his medical condition so complex that everyone had done—and was doing—everything they could, but something was going very wrong with him, and I refused to be quiet about it. I took her advice, and I went and caught a few hours' sleep, and when the doctors made their rounds the next morning, I was a force of nature. I was polite but loud. I told them I refused to let them give my son the drug because something else was going on, and I wanted it all checked again by every single specialist.

Corbin was three months old, and I was tired, but I stood firm between the doctors and my son and told them to do it all again, every test on every organ until they found the cause. They compromised with me. They would take him off the drug for forty-eight hours and see what happened. In the meantime, they would get everything looked over again. I could have hugged them; I was so relieved. I felt that I was right, and I just needed a second set of eyes to look over all these notes again and find it; there had to be something else making him so unwell. I would have felt empowered, but it was too soon to call, and I had yet to get the answers back. Sure enough, within a few hours, we had the cardiac team appear, and new tests were run at his bedside, a different doctor then ordered a lumbar puncture, and we started to work through the list. I knew then they were taking me seriously, and I suddenly realised that I had a voice—one that might make a difference to his situation.

The next day a confident lady strode through the doors with a team of doctors following her, she held Corbin's bulging medical folder under her arms, and her demeanour showed she meant business. I liked her instantly.

She introduced herself as the head of the gastro team, and this was the first time I had ever met a female who was so accomplished in such a specialised and highly complex field. I have met more since, but this lady was the first, and she made a heck of an impact on me. To this day, I admire her intelligence and professionalism. She seemed to take me seriously and sat me down and asked me to go through everything. She wanted to see the notes I had diligently been taking over the past few months, every test taken, results given, and everything in between. She asked if she could take a biopsy when he headed into surgery later that evening to have new access lines put in his veins, as they were struggling to get a cannula in anymore. I agreed instantly, happy that at least everyone was trying. I sat outside the theatre doors for the umpteenth time and kissed his head as he emerged later that evening and then headed back home to my bed for the first time in days.

The next day was Friday 6 May, two days before Mother's Day. As I walked into the ward early that morning, the gastro team was already waiting for me by Corbin's bedside, and they were listening intently to what the doctor was telling them. I raced over to see what was happening, and she said she needed me to take a seat. Now, this was a new one, as I had never really been asked to take a seat before—and I had been given all sorts of news that made my knees buckle beneath me—so this instantly made my chest tighten. She explained the test results had come back from the biopsy, and there was a problem with his liver. Corbin had a rare chronic liver disease called biliary atresia, which was causing the many unexplained medical relapses.

I was elated, as we had finally found what was wrong, which meant that we could now work in the right direction to fix the issue. But it was soon explained to me this new diagnosis, when added to Corbin's already extensive medical problems, was not one that could be just stabilised with medication. It was a lot more serious than I could have ever imagined. He would need to undergo a surgery called a Kasai procedure, which essentially brings up part of his intestines and attaches them to the liver to drain the bile away, because his bile ducts were not functioning.[5] It was something he had been born with, and it explained his recurring jaundice.

It was very serious surgery, and it was urgent. Corbin needed to go in for surgery as quickly as possible. There were diagrams drawn in an attempt to show me what it meant. They talked of needing a liver transplant further down the track and mentioned that no-one could guarantee the surgery would be successful as he was already very weak. I tried to take it all in, I really did. I took that diagram home, and I researched organs and how they worked, and I just felt like my head was spinning with facts that I was desperately trying to process fast enough so I could be helpful in some way. Part of me kept thinking just how happy I was we had a piece of hope. We finally had an answer, even if it was one I didn't want to hear. It meant that even if that chance was 1%, we were still in the game.

Corbin had improved immensely since the diazoxide had been removed from his system; he was back to breathing on his own again. I was able to make encouraging phone calls to Ben and family and tell them we had answers and an option to fix it and it was going to be okay, I knew it was. The surgery was scheduled for three days later,

Monday 9 May, which would also allow me to share Mother's Day with him.

I thought this was wonderful and I wasn't absorbing just how serious this was. In the afternoon, the doctor and the ward coordinator called Ben and me into the office to sit down and talk. In the three months we had been there, this had never happened. I was a little surprised as I figured we had this all under control now. It turns out my ability to focus on the positives had rendered me naïve to the seriousness of our situation. In the office, they went through step by step what having biliary atresia meant, that if—and it was an *if*— the Kasai procedure was successful, this would be a lifelong concern. Basically, we were going to be buying ourselves some time here.

The specialists in the office said this in a much more educated and gentle manner, but the easiest way I can describe what our situation was in my non-medical way is: the earlier biliary atresia is detected and treated with a Kasai procedure, the higher the survival chance. The longer it takes to find and treat, the more permanent damage is caused to the liver, and the likelihood of the Kasai being successful is lessened. So firstly, you need to have undergone surgery as early as possible, preferably before eight weeks. Then you hope it actually works and the bile drains away as expected. After this, you still can have complications arise at any time, which means having an early liver transplant. Then you have to hope that if you do require a transplant, you get a match in time, and then you pray that the body can accept it.

Now because we had so many other organs causing issues and we didn't find out about this until now, Corbin was not the desired eight-to-ten weeks old, but fourteen weeks old. Scans showed he already had cirrhosis and portal hypertension. There was a chance that he might not make it through the surgery, but even if he did, what would follow could never be guaranteed.

As the reality set in, I remember throwing myself over the desk sobbing, telling them that my son had never even had a chance to know what he was fighting for; how was he going to make it through this risky surgery? The odds were against him, and us, and I just couldn't hold it in anymore.

I sobbed and wailed how this was just not fair; Corbin only knew a life of pain and horrible procedures, and I was hysterical.

Why would he keep fighting when all he has known is pain, just pain? This is just a life of torture, this not fair for him. I was hysterical for the first time since he was born, truly inconsolable, and with gut-wrenching sobs, I fell into a heap. How could he possibly want to keep fighting when he didn't have any idea there was this other incredible life outside these doors awaiting him? 'I can't lose him; I can't.'

I don't recall much more of what happened in there; I remember that Ben kept asking questions as he still struggled to understand what was happening, and because he wasn't at the daily doctors' meetings, he hadn't been able to learn the medical terms as I had. Still, there was no denying what they were telling us, and my body finally couldn't take anymore. Ben almost carried me out of the ward with my racking, heaving lungs and floods of tears streaming. I had no control over any emotion as my body shook at the horror of it all.

We went down to the carpark and opened the back of our station wagon and sat there. Unable to hide my distress, I cried uncontrollably as cars leaving and entering the hospital car park kept stopping and asking if we needed help, and we just kept waving them away, lost in our grief.

We pulled ourselves together enough to go back in to see Corbin and say goodbye until the morning, and then I sobbed the whole way home, huddling into the corner of the car seat as though my heart was surely being ripped out of my chest.

On Mother's Day, we were very quiet on the drive to the hospital. It is a hard day to celebrate when you are in NICU. Upon entering the ward, the doctors smiled as they said they had organised a surprise for us. They were going to help me show Corbin what he was fighting for before his surgery the following day. As I made my way to his cubicle, I saw grins in my direction from the other parents who looked longingly to see my reaction. I had no idea what was going on, but clearly, everyone else did. We got to his cubicle, and there stood the most beautiful sight I had ever seen. Our dear friend and superhero nurse, Shannon, stood with portable monitoring units and a pram. They had managed to get permission for Corbin to leave the hospital that had been his home for fourteen weeks. With a senior nurse and lots of equipment in tow, I could take my son outside to the park directly across the road from the hospital. I had a twenty-minute time limit from the moment we left the ward, but the joy the news gave me was immeasurable. The other parents who had witnessed our lows the days prior were so excited for us, and I couldn't stop smiling as I tucked my little boy into a pram for the first time. Together with the fantastic nurse who helped make this possible (thank you, Corinne!), I pushed my son outside so that he could feel the warm sun on his face and the breeze against him for the first time.

He could hear the trees rustling in the wind, children playing on the swings, and the smell of the grass. It was the most amazing twenty minutes in months. We were together, outside of the sterile—and at times, claustrophobic—walls. Rhyz got to hold his brother for as long as he wanted. Although the fact that Corbin's most life-risking surgery to date was happening the following morning and never far from my mind, it was the most beautiful Mother's Day I could have imagined.

CHAPTER 10

CARRY ON MY WAYWARD SON

Corbin's Kasai surgery was going to be his most complicated procedure to date, and a talented surgeon who was known for performing the impossible was tasked with the responsibility of making his liver functional. By this stage, I had developed a routine that I did for good luck more than anything. There were a few items that went through the theatre doors with Corbin on his previous successful surgeries, and I made sure that—although they likely were removed due to sterile concerns—they were still placed at the foot of his bed each time he made his way into the theatre.

Those items included a bright blue muslin wrap. Folded inside was a tiny sock that had belonged to Rhyz when he was a newborn, with a little curl of Rhyz's first haircut tucked inside its toe. It held a set of three Chinese coins Ben had been handed by a total stranger from her handbag when he was on shift at work one day. He was devastated to have been missing yet another day at his son's bedside, and a lady overheard him talking to others about the dire state of Corbin. She then reached into her handbag and handed him these three lucky coins, joined with red ribbon, and pushed them into his palm. They had stayed tucked next to Corbin's hospital bed ever since and became part of the 'good luck' package that was formed in the early days. A small pink rose quartz heart was added, and it was all neatly tagged and bundled together and brought out for days such as this.

I remember every moment after I kissed his little forehead goodbye and signed the consent forms that saw him whisked away to a team of specialists awaiting him. Ben and I were guided back out to the surgical waiting room, which was to the direct right of the main theatre doors. These waiting rooms were filled with parents and children, biding their time until their name was called. Days like these I found the hardest; the feeling like someone had reached in and was physically squeezing your chest was overwhelming. It took everything I had not to scream at the sky to make the world alright again.

I sat in the room with a book clutched in my hands that I couldn't bring myself to read and I listened to the mumblings of everyone around me who were going about their daily lives and tried to keep it together. One mother and her teenage son, whose leg was in a cast, were making themselves known to the room, loudly venting their frustration to anyone within earshot that his procedure had been delayed. It was times like this that have kept me aware in life that you never know what the person next to you is going through. Choose your words and expressions very carefully because you never know who is trying their best to hold it all together while they are standing right beside you looking perfectly fine.

That mother and her son only knew their frustration that day. The fact they had been delayed (likely due to my son or a case very similar) was not something they could comprehend. I, on the other hand, saw them as lucky. To know that your medical issue was not critical and could be 'pushed back' was a luxury we never had. They couldn't see the reason they were delayed was so that another family could maybe spend a few extra hours with their loved one.

As I looked around and saw people more closely and wished I was in their shoes, I couldn't stay in the room a moment longer. The air was stifling me. I felt like I was being taunted by all these healthy children and families, with their total lack of consideration about how grateful they should be for what they had and the fact they would never see it was too much to take at that moment. I told a kind old lady, who was volunteering her time behind the reception desk that I needed to leave the room and I would be sitting outside the theatre doors if any phone calls came in from the doctors inside.

We were told that it might take around four to five hours, and I refused to move until I saw Corbin come out through those doors again. I sat cross-legged on my jacket against the wall watching with nervous anticipation as the doors would open and close, allowing other surgeons in and out of the main double doors leading into the surgical theatres. I sat, and I sat, and I sat. As the hours ticked by so painfully slow, I thought about the bunch of flowers delivered to me on the ward the day before for Mother's Day. There was a card, but it had no name attached to identify the sender. It simply read 'Happy Mother's Day'. I had spent the evening asking staff if they knew who had sent me such a thoughtful gift, but no-one knew. I'd lived in a bubble for so long that, outside the hospital walls, all but a few of my friends had drifted away.

I looked at other mothers who sat with their children on life support, and each day they were comforted by their own mother. I didn't have that. For a long time, I hadn't wanted her in my life; the choices made on her behalf as a mother was something I could never forgive or understand. But in that small window of my darkest hour, as I watched our son fighting for life, I wished my mother was like the others in the NICU. If we were ever going to reconnect, then that time in my life would have been it. I hadn't needed her previously, but when those flowers arrived, there was a twenty-four hour period that I saw a glimmer of hope. I just needed it so badly.

I was aware that my immediate family—who I had not had any contact with for years—were aware of our situation, due to random contact with distant relatives in New Zealand. A little piece of me ached to have someone reach out. As I sat and looked at those hospital walls, I had a phone call from Ben's mum, Anne, who, along with Ben's sister, Sarah, had been with us every step of the way. While she was calling to see how we were holding up, she mentioned that she hoped I had received the flowers they had sent me yesterday, and I welled up in appreciation. It was that exact moment I decided I would never have my mother's name again touch my lips. It was an unforgivable final betrayal, and I would never change my stance. Growing up, when I would question something, I would be met with 'When you are older, you will understand'. But as I grew, I understood less. My love for my children is without limits.

I love them endlessly, and I am so proud that I am no reflection of how I grew up: surrounded by falsehoods, secrecy, and manipulation. Someone once asked me if I was nervous about becoming a mother so young, and I said 'absolutely not' without hesitation. I knew I would make a great mother, that I would be— and am—selfless when it comes to parenting. My children always come first. I am sure many people would argue this point, saying mothers need to put themselves first, but I disagree. It works for me, and I certainly don't consider myself a martyr by doing so. I chose to be a mother. I live and breathe for my children alone. No age, distance, or miscommunication would ever dampen my fierceness and dedication to protecting them and being there in whatever way they need me.

My children would never be used as pawns in egotistical games between warring divorced parents, and I would always be there for them with boundless, unquestionable love. I realised then that Ben's entire family was now my family. They showed up time and time again to be there in their grandson's and nephew's most life-changing moments. It is funny what lessons you take from experiences such as this. I became a changed woman from the person who walked through those hospital doors months prior. I was unforgivingly different and would steadfastly remain so ever after.

Ben kept himself distracted by going for short walks and getting coffee, but I couldn't move. I felt stuck in place, and as five hours came and went without a word from the surgical theatre, I started to get restless.

I watched as other parents went through the doors to see their children off to surgery and I stayed in place long enough to see them being wheeled out again after. Yet I remained, waiting for a sign of hope. After about six hours, a kind volunteer, who had been bringing cups of tea into the hallway for me all day, came out and asked me to take a phone call from the theatre in the waiting room office. Over the phone, the surgeon reassured me Corbin was stable, but it would be another hour or so until completion. He wasn't able to give any further details but wanted to ask my permission for Corbin to have another blood transfusion while he was under as he was struggling a little in that area. I gave my consent immediately and then resumed my wait by the theatre doors, quietly calming myself as best I could.

Nurses from Corbin's NICU ward came throughout the day and brought me chocolate Freddo® frogs and a sandwich and would sit with me while on their break and ask for any updates. When eight hours came, I was informed by a doctor from Corbin's ward that they were just taking Corbin out of anaesthesia. They expected to be able to move him from the theatre back to NICU within thirty minutes. I was told what to expect and made aware he was frail, but they had managed to perform the Kasai. Only time would tell if it was successful. Not to do things in halves, it was discovered once his liver was examined that his blockages were not at the expected part of the bile ducts, which would be the part that connects directly to the liver. Instead, his duct had died at the other end, which was less common.

They couldn't say if this would be to his detriment, and at this stage, I didn't much care for further bad news and hung my hopes on that 1% rule: if there was a 1% chance he might make it through, then that 1% could be us. I have clung to this from the first day we started our journey. It didn't matter how bad the odds happened to be, the fact we were still going and still breathing (even if a machine was doing it for us) gave me hope, and that was all we needed. When the theatre doors opened, there was a team swarming his bed, and they rushed directly back to his spot on the main floor of 6B where another team awaited their arrival.

I sprinted after them and tried to listen to the handover notes between specialists as he was hooked back up to the machines on the ward and disconnected from the portable devices. He was back on life support and heavily sedated and looked painfully swollen all over. His stomach had a dressing that covered a neat, straight incision that went from one side of his stomach to the other, and every arm and leg had cannulas in place pumping various medications back into his tiny body. But he had survived the surgery, and as I kissed his forehead again, I told him to hold tight, he would get better now, and we would soon be home together.

It took a couple of weeks for him to bounce back from this procedure, but every day with the nurses we played 'blood test lotto'; a great game to pass the time where we would guess various blood level results and see who got close to the accurate answer. Every day, his jaundice levels dropped, and his blood sugars never dipped again. We were coming closer to stabilising, and every day was a step in the right direction. He still couldn't manage to swallow without aspirating, so nasogastric feeds continued. Every four hours, he had small feeds to keep his body going. I had learnt how to control all the extra equipment that I imagined I would one day be bringing home with us. I was very confident in being able to change dressings, administer meds and feeds, and keep on top of recording his stats, heart rate, and temperature regularly.

I started to organise everything in our new home so when we did come out of the hospital, we would be able to reassemble his nursery that once stood waiting for him in our old house. I wanted to reclaim some of the time and experiences we had lost as a family and bringing him to our own home was so important. I had found a lovely, old house near Fremantle, and with the help of some dear friends, we managed to get the move done in one day, freeing up my evening to spend back by my son's side at the hospital. We were quickly running out of savings at this point, using what we had to move again and keep maintaining the car to do the long, daily hospital commutes. Ben was still working long hours to bring in extra money to assist us, but I was unable to go back to work. Our income had halved at this stage. We weren't struggling yet, but we knew things were getting tight. Still, we kept our chins high and soldiered on. With Corbin improving by the day, and Rhyz looking forward to celebrating his upcoming eleventh birthday, we were positive and resilient.

I started to make sure I was able to look after myself and my mental health in this highly stressful situation, and I began to work out in the mornings before I attended the hospital. I employed a personal trainer and started to lift weights twice a week. It helped boost the serotonin levels I knew would surely begin dropping at some stage, and it made me feel like I had a way of releasing my frustrations at the world after a tough week watching my son fighting for his health. Lifting heavy weights would, from that day, become my way to rebalance myself when the pressure was on. When I started lifting, I soon realised that when I was concentrating on not dropping weights on my head, I was unable to think of anything else. It was the only time my mind would clear. The rest of the time, the worry and the constant fear hung heavily on me, weighing me down.

I also decided I was going to get my family's initials tattooed on my wrist in a delicate handwritten script. I had my sons' and Ben's initials etched onto my left wrist; I wanted to take a permanent action that showed my little family was always together, although, at the time, it wasn't able to happen in person. I held everything together, as best I could. I was pulled in a million directions, and the maternal guilt was never soothed. I felt like I was betraying Rhyz when I would bring him to the hospital and leave him to wait with his homework in the reception of 6B while I visited his brother. And I felt terrible when I left Corbin on life support in the ward and went home to pick up Rhyz from school. I couldn't win. However, it was yet another learning curve, as I didn't have an option. Each day, I knew I tried my best to be there for everyone. I learnt to stop feeling so guilty for not being perfect or being able to give everyone 100% of me. I knew I was doing my best, certainly given the circumstances, and I started to see myself in a different light. I realised how strong I could be. I was able to face a mother's worst fear every day and still get up and keep going for everyone. The life I was living was one I always imagined happened to other people; it certainly didn't happen to people like me. Yet here I was, and I was standing staunch in the face of a nightmare and didn't blink. I held on to hope desperately and did everything I could to keep spirits up for myself and my family.

Each morning, the doctors made their rounds and discussed how we would proceed. One particular morning as they came close to us, a nurse came up to me smiling broadly as I cradled my son. She whispered to me, 'The doctors are going to see if Corbin can go home next week.' For the first time in my life, I cried tears of joy. I sobbed with fat tears rolling down my smiling face, holding him so close to me, not realising how much I had longed to hear those words I think deep down, I feared I might never have. I never understood what it meant when people would say they 'cried tears of joy', but that day I was the poster child for it; I had never been so elated. I never allowed myself to think anything but positive thoughts, but deep down, my soul ached from trying to keep my head up, sometimes without any substantial reason.

I couldn't believe it. The date was set for the Monday after Rhyz's birthday celebrations, and as soon as the doctors confirmed the news, we started organising what would need to happen before he was discharged. A nurse would come to our house daily to continue administering medication into Corbin's permanent line, as we weren't allowed to do this ourselves. We would get boxes of medical tape, syringes, and all his prescriptions, and we would soon be able to start finding our feet. Cartons of special medical milk, prescribed as a food supplement, were packed into our linen cupboard, and a sterile medication station was set up to ensure no contamination when I drew up the multitude of Corbin's daily medicines.

The day came before I knew it. Twenty weeks after being admitted into hospital on February 1, we finally experienced the high of leaving the incredible world of NICU Ward 6B. I felt overwhelming gratitude to every doctor and nurse who made it possible for us to reach that point and pure adrenaline-driven excitement for bringing home our littlest family member for the first time. The day we said our goodbyes and took the last steps through the doors was so hard to describe. It was surreal as to wait and hope for something so badly that you can barely risk saying it out loud in case you jinx it in some way, and the feeling that it had all come to fruition was desperately overwhelming.

With the first doctor's appointment set a couple of days after Corbin's discharge, we were fully prepared for what was to become our new daily life outside of the hospital. I set up Corbin's cot beside our bed; we were going to be coming home to four-hourly feeds that would run through his nasogastric tube, and each feed had to run for thirty to forty-five minutes to try to counteract any aspiration issues.

I had done my research, and due to long term ventilation and nil by mouth, I was greatly concerned about Corbin developing oral aversions. So every feed was done only after he was offered a bottle. He still was unable to suck correctly and never showed any interest or signs of hunger. He was then made to sit up and suck his dummy while the feed ran so that he would hopefully get used to understanding the connection between moving his mouth and his stomach feeling full. It was a routine that was somewhat intimidating, but to make sure that I never missed one of the eight medications given to him up to four times daily, I kept a book and recorded each feed, medicines, temps, heartrates, and all the notes in between. Having Corbin home was simply indescribable. The sleep deprivation was brutal, but the fact that I was no longer spending up to five hours on the road in transit was a huge help. The poor, old, white Magna® wagon we were using had worn out a long time ago. It chugged along as best it could, but the daily miles had worn the tyres thin, and we booked in to have them replaced only a couple of days after Corbin came home.

There was a small tyre shop in Fremantle, a family run business right next to the Norfolk Hotel on South Terrace near our home, and we were nervous about going out in public with Corbin. I had come prepared with all his syringes, medical equipment, and everything we needed to last us the short period while the tyres were replaced. I recall that by this stage we had very little money left. Centrelink had continued to delay my maternity payments or even acknowledge that we were in dire straits and assist with processing carer payments, even though paperwork had been lodged within weeks of Corbin's birth.

It meant that while we lived on Ben's wage, we used all the savings we had to pay for moving costs, daily travel to the hospital, and all the new additional expenses we suddenly faced. We could only afford to buy two new tyres at this stage, and we went for a short walk while they were fitted to our reliable, old car. We were so nervous about Corbin catching anything that I stayed at a distance with the pram and never ventured into the office at all. I had bought a plastic rain cover that I fitted to the pram, which at least stopped people leaning in to see him or touch him. We kept him as protected as we could.

We had managed to hook up Corbin's portable pump and milk tube to the back of the handle, which allowed us to continue to feed him while we moved around. When we returned, we promised we would call soon to book in for the remaining tyres, and while Ben paid in the office, I unhooked Corbin's devices and moved him gingerly back into his car seat, then made our way home.

We mustn't have been home more than thirty minutes when Ben's mobile rang in the bedroom. I could hear him as he answered and immediately grew concerned as his voice cracked while he started to respond to whoever was on the phone. He spent a few minutes trying to keep his composure while he finished a very one-sided conversation. After he got off the phone, he was quite beside himself. After he was able to pull himself together, he explained what had happened. When he was inside paying for the tyres, the lady who owned the business saw me in the background manoeuvring Corbin who, due to the obvious tubing on his face and little bandaged arm, was quite clearly a little under the weather. She had inquired about him, and Ben had given a brief overview of our situation.

Once we left, she spoke to her husband, and they had decided they would do something that would mean more to us than they could ever know. They had called to let us know our money was being refunded back into our account. They had also organised to have our other two tyres ready for us, and they wanted us to return as soon as possible as they were gifting them to us. They wanted to help, and they wanted to give us hope. We could barely breathe for sobbing. The thought that someone would do something so generous for us without even knowing us at all was incomprehensible, overwhelmingly so.

It was the most beautiful gesture, and one we so badly needed. Knowing that perfect strangers in the community weren't going to let us struggle alone was the glimmer of hope that we would be alright.

That small gesture would pave the way for something incredible many years later; the ripple effect was in full force here, even though it wouldn't be known for quite some time.

In the meantime, we started getting into our newly formed routine. Corbin had a review appointment back at the hospital only a few days after he was discharged, and I was so excited heading in there to let them know how well we were travelling. When I walked into the doctor's office, he looked at Corbin for a little bit longer than he should have and started to ask me queries relating to any symptoms he may have been displaying. I was so confused; Corbin looked fine to me. He was tolerating feeds, medications, and sleeping well.

The doctor unwrapped Corbin from his blanket and kept pointing out things to me I still couldn't see. I started to cry. I had no idea what I was supposed to be seeing. What was I missing? The doctor ordered some blood tests and explained Corbin was showing signs of infection again. I couldn't understand it; he was already on antibiotics and had shown no signs of fever or discomfort. I was lost, it was my job to look after him, and I had arrived so confident that

I was doing everything right, only to be told I had missed all the signs I needed to see.

Within the hour, the blood tests had come back with heightened infection levels, and they explained how my son would once again be admitted back into the hospital he had left not even a week earlier. I crumbled internally. *How did I miss it? It was up to me to see the signs, and I didn't. Maybe I couldn't care for him at all properly? How was I going to be able to keep him alive?*

This time, we were heading to the paediatric ward, and at that moment, I had no clue this would become our second home for the foreseeable future. What was initially a minor infection would continue to flare up and then disappear again. Because we were already under antibiotic cover, most times it was hard to pinpoint where the infection originated. Sometimes it would be reoccurring chest infections, other times it would be gastro-type symptoms. Still, the result was the same regardless of the diagnosis: Corbin turned into a frail baby who spent the majority of his life in hospital, undergoing more tests and procedures and hooked up to various machines again to assist feeds, breathing, and provide everything from pain relief to fluids every waking moment; this went on for months.

We had previously thought we were going to be making a new start after we exited 6B at the end of June. Before we knew it, it was coming close to Christmas, and we had spent nearly an entire year in the hospital. By the end of the year, I was panicking. We just didn't seem to be making ground, and as a family unit, we were beginning to struggle. The daily hospital trips, the endless worry, and the lack of respite for Corbin, or us, for the foreseeable future, was tightening in on us.

The concerns that the recurring infections were ascending cholangitis (an expected but unwanted infection of the liver) had started to become a genuine concern with everyone. With his declining health and all the symptoms in place, the diagnosis became our worst fear. The doctors' concern that the liver transplant might be needed sooner than expected started being a subject on the rounds in the mornings.

It was all becoming incredibly serious, and we were trying our hardest to remain as positive as possible. Ben's family took turns in making sure a family member was with us nearly every moment of the journey. I have no idea how they did it, but I would have been lost without them. They would sweep in from Victoria and buy groceries and clean the house, all the while helping in every way possible to keep us going. Ben and I started to struggle to communicate our pain to one another at that point. Understandably, the pressure of two parents undergoing such trauma together did cause us to lose our way a little. I felt resentful that he wasn't able to be there with me during such heart-breaking moments. I knew he was doing his absolute best, but everyone handles their grief in different ways. It is hard to explain unless you have experienced it yourself, but sometimes the pain that comes from such a raw place can make it hard to find your connection again. Ben would unwind with a few drinks each night after work with his friends, and I would be doing the juggle between hospital and home and feeling increasingly isolated with my pain. We knew we had issues between us, but we also consistently put our children and their needs first so that we could all cope as well as possible. Rhyz started spending school holidays in Wodonga with Ben's family. It gave him a break from the stress at home, and he was able to be spoilt and have the attention he deserved lavished upon him. Ben's sister, Sarah, had been gently mentioning the new Melbourne hospital that was being completed when she would visit and tried to keep our hopes up by letting us know we always had other options. The thought of moving to a different hospital had never entered our minds—we were so caught up in the daily challenge that we were blinkered to other options, and the fear of the unknown kept us firmly in our place.

However, this soon came to a head after Corbin had a horrifying bout of sepsis that had gone undiagnosed and saw him moments from the edge. I stood my ground and literally screamed for help from other wards. A doctor was called down from the intensive care unit, and he instantly diagnosed him and whisked Corbin into the safety of NICU. At this stage, I lodged a complaint, and not long after received a formal apology from the hospital. To this day, I can't bring myself to discuss it openly.

Watching him waste away and hearing a rattle coming from his chest as his sunken eyes slowly faded was single-handedly the worst experience of any of our hospital experiences to date. For the first time in almost a year of Corbin's treatment, I was quickly losing faith with the people in charge of his care.

The gastro team had decided the time had come to sit down and discuss the next step regarding a liver transplant. The meeting was set, and I was ready. I knew I had never been healthier. I didn't drink or smoke, and I was young and fit. I was more than willing to donate a portion of my liver. I knew I would be an easy match; I had sat by Corbin during the blood transfusions of his O+ blood type, so I knew we shared the same blood type. To me, that was the first step sorted.

I remember walking into the office that morning and making small talk as I was told how we would end up travelling to either Sydney or Melbourne as that is where infant liver transplants were being performed. I thought that was going to be fine; we would go and stay with Ben's family in Wodonga. They explained how we would be able to do conference calls to the surgeons before we made the big move to Melbourne, and we discussed the rest of the testing process to make sure I was a perfect match. Then, as the specialist started to take notes in the folder, I noticed on the inside of the cream cover was a bright red notation.

It had an 'A+' written in bold. I remember seeing it and instantly interjected, pointing at the letter and asking what that was. The specialist looked up at me and said, confused, that it was Corbin's blood type. I shook my head and explained how it wasn't; we had the same blood type; it was O+. I had seen the bags of blood labelled. There was silence in the room as the specialist said to me slowly that

A+ patients are able to receive transfusions of O+ blood, but it didn't mean they had the same blood type themselves.

I was so confused. From the moment we had known about Corbin's liver, the doctors and I believed that I was the match who could donate if it came to it. Now that we were here, it turns out this belief had been false. As I sat there, the specialist kept trying to figure out where we had got this wrong and tried to console me with the fact that Corbin and Ben's family shared the same blood type and we could discuss being a donor with them.

I could barely get the words out as my mind just started to collapse in on me. Ben and his family have a medical history of lupus, and the moment the words came out of my mouth, the specialist just sank back into his chair. Corbin's blood type, and therefore the perfect donor match, lay in a bloodline that was unable to donate at all due to their genetic autoimmune disease.

I can't save my son, I thought. This situation was now entirely out of my control, and if his liver did fail, he would be at the mercy of someone passing away at the correct time to save him. Not only that but now we needed someone who had his A+ blood type. The odds were stacking up, and I can remember making it only halfway down the stairwell after that meeting before breaking down on the phone to Ben's mum.

'I'm not his blood type, I can't save him,' I wailed in the stairwell as people passed me with sympathetic looks that I was getting used to being shown. 'I can't help him at all!' My whole body shook from grief.

I had to wait until Ben was on his lunch break to tell him. It was becoming harder and harder to get through these appointments alone. Still, no matter how much I protested that he had plenty of holidays accumulated, Ben insisted it was better to save them for the dire emergencies. I had stopped trying to convince him that this was all dire and accepted that we each were trying our best just to make it through the days.

But the liver transplant options were a blow we never saw coming. I do not know how I had continued to know every small detail about our son's health but confused the blood type.

Within forty-eight hours, Ben and I decided we were going to pack up everything we had, leave our old lives behind and take our chances in a Melbourne hospital. The liver transplant team had already explained that paediatric liver transplants are only handled in either Sydney or Melbourne, and we needed help, quickly. He barely survived the late-diagnosed sepsis and reoccurring cholangitis, and we couldn't keep going on like this.

Two weeks fresh out of the NICU, we bought plane tickets and packed up our house. With a referral to a follow-up paediatrician letter in my possession, we boarded a plane with an oxygen tank and flew to Melbourne.

CHAPTER 11

EVERYTHING HAS CHANGED

It turns out having previous experience starting over in a strange new town came in very handy for me in the next sudden adventure of my life. Wodonga, located on the border of New South Wales, was not somewhere I had envisioned moving to, but when you are desperate to get help for your son, you will not even think twice about taking every chance. The safety of Ben's family was perfect as it would provide a home base for Rhyz when Corbin needed treatment and further surgeries.

I thought about all of this on the smooth flight over. After we landed, we drove into what was to be my new hometown for the first time. I saw gorgeous trees and flowers that seemed to bloom everywhere across the rolling hills. I caught myself thinking, *If I'm going to live anywhere, then this is a pretty incredible place to be.*

We had left knowing there were still quite a few operations in our future, and with the liver playing funny games, we knew it was in everyone's best interests to be over there already. It was also the year Rhyz was starting high school. I really wanted some normality and routine put back into his life after the hectic year he had been through with all our juggling. Moving east was a solution to that. With such a large, supportive family on arrival, it meant that the home fires would always be burning regardless of where we were, and hopefully, that could take some of the pressure off Rhyz. His hair had just started to grow back in the bald patches the stress-induced alopecia had left, and he was really starting to grow into a wonderful young man. I needed to find a way that would secure both my children's best interests, and this was definitely the answer.

I had no idea what to expect as I hadn't travelled to Victoria before. Rhyz was excited though, as he had previously spent a couple of weeks there during Corbin's hospital stays. While there, he'd learnt a lot about the area. The biggest selling point for him was an Army Cadets base nearby. He'd first shown interest in the army when he was very young, and his enthusiasm had never waned.

The specialist appointment had been booked for two weeks after we arrived. We spent the first two days exploring the neighbourhood with the pram. We also drove past what would be Rhyz's new school; it was due to reopen the following week. Ben had left with his father the previous day; they were driving across the Nullarbor, heading back to Western Australia to collect our faithful Magna and a large trailer packed to the brim with our family belongings.

Unfortunately, Corbin's health declined rather quickly again overnight on the third evening. It seemed that we'd hardly unpacked our bags before Corbin and I had a crash course in admissions at the Royal Children's Hospital Melbourne (RCH).

After racing to the emergency room at the Albury Base Hospital, we were greeted by the best paediatric doctor I have ever met. This doctor met us at the emergency 'crash table' when I raced in with a wheezing and feverish Corbin in my arms. The triage monitors showed his oxygen levels had plummeted to the 70% range, and I was in panic mode. The doctor asked all the right questions, and while he observed this small child with a medical history that belies his age, he turned and asked me why on earth I was in the middle of a small town that has freezing winters. I explained that this was the only way we were going to be able to have the family around to support us. I also remember at that moment seriously wondering, *What the heck have I done? Why did we move here?*

They struggled to stabilise Corbin, and the decision was made to airlift him directly to the RCH. While panic set in, I managed to get hold of Ben before his phone went out of range on his journey to Western Australia. I explained what was happening and that he needed to get back to Melbourne as soon as possible. The realisation that Corbin's health was failing again so quickly was incredibly hard to absorb. Anne and Sarah arrived at the hospital to be with me, and between the flurry of doctors and nurses, we stood in fear.

First, the doctors needed to stabilise Corbin to transport him. After trying and failing to access any veins, which had long been an issue in Perth, they eventually resorted to holding him down as they shaved his fine blonde hair from his head and inserted a cannula into a primary vein in his head. I choked back tears as I helped hold my son's hands away from the electric razor as he screamed in fear, and consoled him as a plastic cup was taped around this precious commodity to make sure it wasn't going to be bumped or pulled out en route.

I looked at his hair as it fell onto the hospital bed sheets and hid my face so my son wouldn't see my tears. I reached out a hand and scooped up what was now his first haircut and held the strands between my fingers. The nurse was kind enough to give me a plastic specimen container to keep the curls. The fact that he had no access to take blood or administer medications was raising alarm bells for the medical staff, and they asked how on earth this had gone in Perth.

I explained it was a disaster there too. If the doctors and nurses were able to get lines in after multiple attempts of trying, then we would be lucky to see the line hold more than twenty-four hours, and if they ever tried to pull back on it to get a blood sample, then it would just collapse the vein instantly. There were frantic phone calls to the waiting Melbourne specialists, and then Sarah was sent to pack a bag for us to take before the ambulance drove us to the airfield.

Rhyz was fast asleep back in the family home with his uncle as this all unfolded. Sarah promised me she would take over all the meetings in the upcoming week with his new teachers and principal and would organise all his new uniforms and book list that we were meant to get together in the following days. I was so exceedingly grateful for her help, and at the same time, the maternal guilt just kept eating at me. The timing was dreadful, with his poor dad stuck halfway across the Australian desert and me about to board a plane with his brother. It was chaos again. In the early hours of the morning, the ambulance took us out to meet the plane, which quickly whisked Corbin and me up and away to the RCH in Melbourne.

Corbin was breathing on his own aided by oxygen and steroids. Doctors continually monitored his oxygen levels and heart, which was speeding out of control. Now and then, his oxygen would plummet, setting off the alarms inside the small cabin.

A team of doctors and nurses met our stretcher bed as we were finally raced into the entrance of the hospital, and we were ushered into a cubicle in the circular emergency department. There was a central desk in the middle of the room, with glass doors into every cubicle; it was a unique and brilliant design that I had never seen before.

I had now seen so many 'handovers' in my time, I knew the doctors would start going through what they had been informed of. We'd then start to work on what was missing from the puzzle as they tried to grasp the situation in front of them.

A plethora of tests was organised, covering all areas: CAT scans, MRIs, X-rays, and blood, and then once the doctors were in agreement that he was stabilising well, they moved us into the paediatric ICU for observation for the next few hours while they started to get a clearer picture. The hospital had only been opened for two weeks at this stage, and out of the window, I could see the old hospital right next door and a whole lot of scaffolding and walkways that were in place that linked the two buildings.

As we made our way into different departments over the next forty-eight hours completing all the required tests, the nurses would have a giggle at the little things that were happening around us to lighten the mood. We laughed at the elevator doors being poorly timed, so you had to sprint to enter them until maintenance adjusted the timing, and the constant stream of doctors and nurses trying to find the new theatres.

The fish being put in the giant fish tank was terrific to watch, and it was a welcome distraction. This hospital was unlike anything I had ever seen before, gleaming with brand new, state-of-the-art equipment in every room and shiny corridors adorned with exquisite artwork. Everyone had a spring in their step as they moved around in this world-class medical facility.

There was to be a meerkat exhibit in the centre of the waiting rooms. While it was too early for the new inhabitants to be there, it was a remarkable feat and one that, once completed, was a fantastic addition for both parents and their little patients as it was a brilliant distraction from why they may be visiting the hospital. There was a food court with a multitude of restaurants and cafes, lush green grass outside to picnic on, and a walking path that went around the hospital grounds and took in views of the park next door and the tree-lined landscape surrounding the building. To have such an environment to walk out into was so refreshing and instantly lifted my spirits.

With all the test results back, and no conclusive explanation for his drastically low oxygen levels upon admission, the team surrounding him started to work their magic. First, we were moved into a private suite, which was incredible. It was all brand new, and we were the first to occupy this room. It had the prettiest clear-sided cots, a native Australian animal-decorated hospital blanket and matching curtains. In the past year of living predominately inside a hospital, this was a huge difference. I had my own bed built into the room, a small fridge, and a huge window overlooking the trees surrounding the hospital. It changed everything. The doctors in Melbourne worked quickly to organise a team for every area of

Corbin's issues. Before the second day had passed, we had the liver transplant, gastro, respiratory, cardiac, and surgical team, together with dieticians, all focusing on his needs. The first thing that had been deemed high priority was to have Corbin undergo surgery to fit a portacath, which would create instant access for IVs and blood taking. This device would be inserted under the skin near his chest and would have a line running into a main arterial vein to give us all the vein access we needed.

When they realised his first birthday was the next morning, the surgeons actually held off performing the procedure until the following day. On Corbin's first birthday, Anne drove down, and together we sang 'Happy Birthday' with the team of doctors. A makeshift birthday cake was created using a doughnut from the cafeteria. Ben and his dad had managed to make it across the Nullarbor at a record pace, and once they arrived in Perth, Ben boarded the very next flight to Melbourne to meet us at the hospital. He arrived in time to find Corbin healing brilliantly from his successful port surgery, and some of the best specialists in the world dedicated to ensuring that Corbin's health was their foremost concern.

I can remember in those early days at the RCH feeling as though a massive weight had been lifted. We had so many people addressing concerns we had held for so long, and the follow-through with tests and actioning new medications was immediate. I knew the correct decision had been made to move. There was such a long road ahead, and I knew Melbourne was going to be the perfect fit for getting Corbin across the line.

I felt extreme gratitude for the medical treatment he received and how lucky we were to be living in a country that provides such support. Corbin and I ended up staying a little over two weeks after our initial admission. During this time, future surgeries were organised, and specialists put in place. His diet was changed to assist in his much-needed weight gain, and the port was healing nicely under his skin, to provide future vein access in case of emergencies.

Corbin went home from the hospital with a half-shaved head of hair, but I had a heart filled with hope for the future.

Rhyz, in the meantime, had settled quickly into his new high school and, always the easy-going child, had made friends quickly and was enjoying his new surroundings. I found us a small cream and white house with rose bushes decorating the pretty yard, and we moved into our home hopeful about what was coming next. Rhyz had continued to excel at his sports, and I enrolled him in the local soccer team where he flourished even further. Ben had secured himself a position at a local factory working afternoon/night shift, and we started to find our feet in Wodonga, the little town that had a big heart. There were almost weekly appointments at various specialists and therapists while finding my way around our new hometown.

For the first time in my life, I had become self-aware and confident in who I was. I was able to stand proudly and look in the mirror at myself and know that I liked who I was. All the years that I had doubted myself, or had let the uncertainty of other people make me second-guess my abilities, were long gone. The day I walked out of the Perth Hospital after finding my voice to advocate on behalf of my son, I also found a voice for myself. The realisation that life is short and never guaranteed was now at the forefront of my mind. I wanted more than ever to not only give my sons everything they needed in life but also to start going back to my bucket list.

I signed up at the local gym and started back with weight training. On the days that Corbin was stable, I would go for a walk with him in the pram too. I began to spend more time baking and trying new recipes and immersed myself thoroughly in creating a new routine that would have the right balance of creative outlets. I had decided I was going to get a large tattoo art piece on my hip and, in a small break between medical appointments, I started what was to become the best outlet I have ever come across. When Corbin was born the year before, obviously it had been a heck of a ride, and needing to be alert at every moment to provide care for him meant relaxing with a couple of drinks was not going to be an option. The moment I started with what was originally going to be a one-off tattoo, I felt an instant release mixed with a hint of rebellion, and I was hooked.

Before I knew it, I had covered my thighs, stomach, ribs, hips, back, and shoulders with the most beautiful intricate ink filled with 1940's-inspired artwork. I had Latin script designed to read: 'To my sons, I am devoted' as it weaved its way from one shoulder to the other and featured a chandelier dripping jewels that hung from every magical letter. I loved it, and I loved how I looked. Granted, all of my tattoos were able to be hidden easily under any clothing, but I was only getting them for my viewing. They made me feel gorgeous, and Cindy, my artist, wrapped the images around my body to highlight my curves. It was something that was for me alone, and I loved it. After all the years of playing it safe and following the rules, I was starting to let my guard down and find out who I really was.

The cold weather kept us pretty contained to the warmth of the house, and along with the exhausting routine of medical care, I was trying to find myself among what remained. As hard as I tried, there was a loss I felt and couldn't fill, like I was living in a blur of expectations and walking in the footsteps of someone else's life. The burning feeling in my chest of wanting to run headlong into something that soothed my aching heart seemed to keep growing. I had tried so hard to keep everyone upbeat that short of the times we were resuscitating or seeing Corbin being put on life support, I rarely let my strength slip. But I knew it was time to start finding my passion for life again too.

I was feeling, more than ever, just how short the time clock on my life was. There were so many things I thought I had to fulfil. I had finally come out of the dark ages and joined Facebook to keep in touch with Corbin's nurses we left behind in Western Australia. Along with my steadfast friends from Queensland, such as Sam and Trina, I started to realise what a fantastic tool social media was to keep in contact with old friends while living in a different state. I began to feel less alone, and along with my new communication portal of friends, I had also found some gym buddies who I started to share a coffee with now and then.

I worked hard to keep my mental health positive and balance my new lifestyle and felt so proud of the steps I had made to achieve my newfound confidence. Corbin's health was still a daily battle. He had a new diagnosis of epilepsy added to the mix, and this saw a rapid increase of ambulance call-outs followed by quick hospital sprints until the medication dosage was corrected.

There wasn't a month during that first year that didn't see us either in the hospital or in the back of an ambulance. It just didn't let up. The round-the-clock feeding was still being conducted with pumps and nasal tubes, but this situation was eased when Corbin had a permanent stomach tube placed to allow for easier and more comfortable feeds. It was all-consuming, but I had found my small creative outlets. And much like when I was a young, overwhelmed teenage mother, a hot shower, cup of tea, and fresh PJs always seemed to work well to lift my spirits on the long days.

Corbin was fast approaching his second birthday when he had sudden breathing issues and once again was airlifted straight back to Melbourne for priority care. This time, however, his lungs refused to play the game, and he was placed back on life support before he boarded the helicopter. He remained on ventilation for a little over a week. I spent the time by his side, once again promising to whoever was watching over us that I would make it up to them as long as they could help him pull through.

After what felt like the longest time, his lungs began to show signs of improvement, and he started to breathe on his own again. It was another week while he recuperated and regained his strength, and then we finally made our way home. By now, the two years of hospitals had started to take its toll, and I was feeling worn out and bereft of any solace.

I went to the doctor and spoke about how I was starting to struggle emotionally. I finally felt like I had a genuine reason to be able to talk about my emotions, and no longer was I worried that anyone would think I was mentally unsound. I had seen enough parents and carers on the inside of the hospital to know I was handling everything incredibly well, and so when I felt myself slowly sinking, I was able to reach out.

My kind doctor, who knew Corbin's condition, was brilliantly understanding. She diagnosed me with 'situational depression' and explained it was normal, if not expected, for someone in my circumstances to be feeling so low at times. She agreed with my personal view on not wanting to take any medication and suggested maybe it was time I had a couple of nights away to recharge and sleep through the night for the first time in years.

I was incredibly hesitant at first, but after some encouragement from family and friends, I organised a holiday for myself in a few months after Corbin was stable again. In the meantime, I threw my focus onto everyone around me, probably to the detriment of my wellbeing. I decided to hold up my side of the bargain I had made when I was on my knees on the hospital floors talking to the big guy upstairs and began assisting an Australian children's charity, Give Me 5 For Kids®.

I had made a deal with myself and to whoever answered my prayers that I would give back and be a worthy human if my son was spared. I felt like I had to start making my mark to keep Corbin with me.

It was so much easier than I ever imagined; it almost fell into my lap. Firstly, I was asked if I was happy to do some live radio interviews to tell our story and how the Give Me 5 For Kids® charity had helped our family. That was easy. A paediatric life support machine had recently been purchased with funds from this charity for the Albury Base Hospital, and I had seen how important this machine was; I was more than happy to share our experience.

Then I decided I was going to assist in the fundraising that year, which, as it turns out, was made even simpler than I had expected. No-one was willing to turn away a young mother and her child (who was still using his quite obvious nasal feeding tube while his stomach tube healed) when we asked various businesses and schools to come on board with the drive.

A multitude of businesses agreed to take donation buckets in the first week alone, then the local schools agreed to hold separate fundraisers for the cause and it all just snowballed from there. I soon realised so many people wanted to be part of something that helped so many. All they needed was to be asked and shown how to do it. It turns out all those years of planning and being super organised were paying off, and before I knew it, milkshake fundraising stations were being created and free dress days held. It felt incredible to be helping to give back. I finally believed I was doing good and repaying my debt to society for saving my son.

Rhyz's high school came on board. First, his soccer team and then his cricket team all pitched in, and no-one even blinked an eyelid at the tiny teetering toddler who wore his Queensland State of Origin Jersey around Victoria and NSW while he helped collect the donations. It was fantastic.

I recall standing in my kitchen one day, and my phone pinged an alert. The moment I opened the message, my heart almost stopped. There was Joel's name across my screen. I instantly felt my chest tighten as I suddenly recalled the years of teen angst over our teenage relationship and the pain it felt to have to leave him all those years ago. He had found me on social media after nearly fifteen years, and he wanted to call me. I didn't even have the words at the time, and I remember heading out for my daily run. I clocked my fastest time yet! It seemed like I couldn't outrun my past though. I had no idea what to expect; it had been so long. I had never even mentioned Joel to Ben; talking to anyone about my past was something I couldn't do. It felt too raw, even after all this time. I kept opening the message, re-reading it, and not knowing how to reply. It took me the better part of the day to send my number through and almost instantly, my phone rang.

I inhaled sharply, and a jolt went through me as I stared at this unknown number as it flashed across my screen. The moment I picked up and heard Joel's voice, I was taken back to all those years ago: the nights spent laughing as he tried to teach me how to smoke a cigarette while we sat hidden in the laneway next to the bus stop, and when we picked out his suit and my formal gown so he could attend his graduation as a guest of honour, even though he didn't complete the year. All those memories came flooding back in a heartbeat. He sounded the same: his laugh, his words; I could see him vividly in my mind. We spent an hour catching up on what we had missed in each other's lives over the years. He was a proud dad and had stayed in our hometown as he had always wanted to.

We spoke about friends we had lost contact with, plans that hadn't entirely gone our way, and just what a strange ride this life turned out to be. Before we hung up, he said that he had tried to find me—that all those years ago, he had called the number to my father's house in Western Australia after I had gone in to have the abortion and was told in no uncertain terms he was never to contact me again. That was the part of the conversation that hurt the most, and my voice cracked as I tried to say goodbye.

CHAPTER 12

TORN

When Ben came home from work that night, I explained the phone call to him and how I thought I was ready to reach out to a couple of other people from my past and face a few things I felt I needed some closure on. It was a strange thought as I had managed to push it all aside just to keep my head above water for those early years and not mourn the loss of what was. Now, suddenly, I wanted to face everything head-on.

I had a friend request pending from Janette, who I had lost contact with many years prior. I knew she had been still loosely associated with my mother back then, and I didn't want to bring any negativity from that toxic relationship into my family's life. I sent her a quick message explaining I would love to be in contact with her, but if my mother was still a part of her life, then I sadly couldn't do it. I received a reply that assured me all communication between them was non-existent, and she would desperately love to be in touch. That was the most heartwarming reconnection that I had. Janette had been the role model of what a mother should be, and I adored her. The fact we were able to find each other after all those years had me squealing with happiness, and instant phone calls between us began.

It cemented my decision, and I started saving for my three-night holiday. I was going to go home. I was going to make everything okay again. I booked my flights for the Anzac Day long weekend and started to count down. Sam and Trina had their baby girl, Scarlett, almost a year after Corbin was born and I was so excited to meet her. Ben and his family made sure everything was in place for the three nights I was to be away, and I boarded my flight absolutely beside myself with excitement. The moment I stepped onto the tarmac, I knew I was home. The air smelled different, and, at that moment, I knew that everything was going to be alright. I had gotten the late flight and had my plans set to meet Janette first thing in the morning, but had barely reached my hotel room when Joel called saying that he was coming over. He was refusing to wait for another second, and I agreed, somewhat nervously, but thrilled at the thought of seeing someone I thought I would never lay eyes on again. He bounded into the room with a bottle of pink champagne and a grin from ear to ear, and I wrapped my arms around him with squeals of excitement.

We laughed and laughed, and after we had gotten over the initial buzz of actually being in the same room again, he insisted we head out and celebrate. We walked the streets where we once had all those years ago and reminisced about everything that had happened. There were apologies and tears and pure happiness that we were no longer at the mercy of adults keeping us apart.

We ran into old school friends, and we all danced, sang, and enjoyed every moment we had together before we said goodbye again. Whether or not we would have been able to make the distance as a couple all those years ago, we would never know. Time had made us take very different paths to each other. I know I was no longer the wild one who matched his crazy antics like we used to together, and he was no longer the Joel I knew either. It didn't matter though, we had closure, and clearly, it was something that we had both needed for a long time.

It wasn't the same love I had left behind, but that was to be expected. We weren't the same people anymore. I don't know how he truly felt about it; he was incredibly respectful of my marriage, but I left feeling that a tiny piece of my heart had been restored—a piece that I hadn't even realised I had left behind. I think a part of me will always carry the old Joel with me. He wasn't the person who had held my heart all those years prior—the person I had, at times, wished would sweep in and save me from the hard life I had been thrust into and whisk me off to the beachfront shack we always dreamed about. But that was okay. The heartache I had felt for so long, mixed with the nostalgia of my old life's hopes, had been soothed.

We all have our paths to travel, and Joel and I had chosen very separate lives to lead. There was nothing between us but platonic love and respect from what we had shared all those years prior.

The next morning saw me leaping into Jen's arms as I surprised her at her workplace with her daughter Kate, who I picked up on the way. We went out for lunch, and I could feel the broken parts of me that had been rejected by my hometown and the situation all those years ago being put back together. There were plenty of tears as we held hands and talked about our children and how regretful we both were that I hadn't accepted her offer to move in with her all those years ago. I didn't know just how badly I had needed this; it was a sentimental time for me. I showed her photos of my sons, and we spoke until the restaurant started to close and then organised to meet again the next day. It was incredible, and I had the feeling that I hadn't been as alone in the world as I always imagined myself to be. People were there, they just weren't able to find me to reach out.

I felt comforted by the memory that I had people keeping a warm thought for me during those lonely, hard nights when I had no-one to turn to. I met Scarlett and hugged Sam and Trina for the longest of times. Their support had been paramount in the past decade, and I missed them dearly. It was fantastic standing in the same room as them and not at the end of the phone for once.

In the weekend I was there, twice I was asked by old school friends if I was going to be seeing Luke. My instant response was 'No'. We had never spoken again after our argument five years earlier, and I didn't feel a need to fix the friendship. He had never tried to contact me, so I let it go and brushed the queries aside.

*

Before I boarded the plane back to Victoria, I made a stop at a tattoo parlour and got myself a tattoo to honour the healing and memories made. It had the word 'Torn', and the postcode of my hometown scribed onto my wrist. It signified how I felt; I was torn, stuck between desperately wanting to go home and the home that I currently had. It was a somewhat cathartic inking, that one. I came back to Victoria with renewed vigour and hope. I sat down with everyone as soon as I got home from the airport and talked a mile a minute as I went over how the landmarks had changed and how fantastic it was. I was on a high, and I wanted more than ever to take my family there now. I wanted to go home. It was time. It all made sense to me now, the feeling lost and not belonging; it was a place—I missed my hometown.

It was time that I went back, let my family grow up on the beaches like I did, and had a team that cheered me on and supported me. Corbin's surgeries were being ticked off, and he was getting stronger by the day, plus the specialist continued to express how much better his lungs would be if we were in a warmer climate. The look on Ben's face said it all; he was not moving. I tried to come to a mutual agreement, that maybe we could move there for a year and then come back. Perhaps we could wait a year and then go? I tried every compromise I could think of, but he wouldn't budge. I felt my heart break a little, but I understood. Wodonga is where he grew up, he was surrounded by his family and friends there, and it was a beautiful town that I also had fallen in love with; it just wasn't *my* hometown.

I hadn't realised how much I needed to have a home team encouraging and supporting me. As incredibly supportive as Ben's family and my new friends were, it wasn't quite the same. Part of me felt that the people I had finally managed to reconnect with were put back in my life at the time I needed them the most, and I badly wanted to have them part of my family's life.

I thought, *Surely, I can wear him down over time.* In the meantime, we had agreed we would alternate taking weekend holidays to catch our breath every six months to keep our sanity. That was enough to keep me sated while I went back to juggling Rhyz's sports and his new position as an army cadet, and Corbin's medical needs.

I cheered Ben at his cricket games, hosted his friends and family for dinners, and tried my hardest to feel like this was my haven. In a way, it was. I had a home with support, and opportunities to start afresh in this small, welcoming town. Excluding the cold weather that played havoc with Corbin's lungs, the medical care was without fault. But the sense that something was missing did not dampen. I had changed, and it was becoming more apparent as time went on. It happened slowly, but the result was someone who wanted to live life a little louder, with a lot more feeling, and I wanted to do it on my terms.

A young doctor who happened to be the head of the paediatric cardiac team in the ICU in Melbourne had left a rather lasting impression on me during one of our stints on life support there. Jodie rounded the door of our cubicle one evening, and from the short sleeves of her bright scrubs were the most incredibly colourful tattoos. Her arms down to the wrists were decorated in vibrant designs that swirled around her, and I couldn't help but admire the artwork.

I remember asking her if having these tattoos affected her career options in any way, as I was heavily tattooed myself, but I had them hidden. I wanted to see if down the track it would be an issue for any future employers. I wanted to know if her senior role was harder to achieve due to the possible discrimination she might have received, and her response was everything I needed to hear. Jodie looked at me with a wide, confident smile. She said she has never had a family member stop her from saving the life of their child because of how she looked and that getting her impressive senior position was based entirely on how hard she worked and how competent she was.

Basically, in a nutshell, she didn't see her tattoos, and neither did those in charge. They only saw her intelligence and dedication to her job; I was amazed. I had always been so shy to change anything outwardly with myself for fear of judgment or to have people think I was a lesser mother or human because I didn't fit into the box correctly. Watching as this woman conducted herself with an air of utmost confidence in herself and her abilities without a second thought for those strangers passing judgement impressed upon me the need to start finding my outward confidence too. I began what would become a mission to add my version of beauty to the outside of me, filling everything I saw on myself and around me with the things that bought me happiness.

My blonde hair soon changed to a soft pastel lilac with victory rolls framing my face. My hidden tattoos started to become visible, and what began with beautiful 1940s artwork on my arm was eventually filled in down to my wrist featuring watercolour bouquets of forget-me-nots, violets, and roses, softly outlined with ribbons. Not only was I changing on the inside, but my true self was evident on the outside as well. That didn't sit well with some people. The new gym friends I had made were quite put off by the changes and made their opinions quite vocal regarding how tacky and cheap these changes made me appear to them.

Years ago, this reaction would have crushed me. Now it meant very little to me; I never needed everyone to like what I was choosing to do with my body. I certainly have no time for people who want to make others feel inferior due to a difference of opinion on what constitutes their version of beauty. I was self-confident in a way I had never been before. I had walked through fire, and I still held my head high. I knew my worth, and I was unshakeable in my self-belief.

Changes also started to appear in my marriage. They had begun to show as we chose different ways of coping with the pain of our son when he was in the hospital back in West Australia, but as our life started to settle in Victoria, those changes became more apparent. I am going to be very delicate with this subject for a multitude of reasons and brush over what needs to be as this has been written not to cause pain, hurt, or humiliation to anyone and Ben is certainly not someone who ever deserves any of that. Before I go any further, I shall reiterate what I have said previously; Ben is the kindest man I have ever met, even to this day. He is loving, generous, funny, supportive, and a devoted father; I loved him, I do still love him, and I always will.

I just, at that stage, realised that while he was everything that is wonderful, he wasn't my soulmate, and I certainly wasn't his. There was no dramatic fighting, no big disappointments, no great story to explain how it changed, it just did. We struggled along for some time, always friends and with a united front, but the previous couple of years had taken their toll and had turned us into different people. We tried very hard to work together, but it was a different love than what we both needed and deserved.

I hoped maybe we could eventually move to Queensland and I would fill that missing piece, and our relationship would find its wings again. I held onto that for quite a few months as we worked together supporting each other and our family. Ben was looking forward to his long weekend break and had chosen to spend his respite time back in Western Australia with the friends we had left the year earlier. He returned refreshed and happy, and we agreed that these few days away every six months were going to be our saving grace to breathe from the unrelenting routine of medical and family commitments we had.

Rhyz had excelled in his school studies and was put in advanced classes to meet his academic requirements. The teachers were discussing the options of allowing him to start university studies while juggling his workload in the upcoming years as he continued to surpass the school curriculum. Everyone was content and fulfilled, and I felt so selfish as I felt so depleted and a little empty. I never lost my positive face, and if I struggled, I'd hide it by crying in the shower where no-one would worry about me.

I thought I should be feeling on top of the world. I had been fighting a battle to keep my son going, and he was spending more time out of the hospital at that stage, yet I felt so guilty that I still wanted something for me. My heart was hurting; something was missing. I had closed all old wounds and made peace with myself over past regrets or mistakes I had made, but that feeling of a piece of the puzzle missing was unrelenting. I looked forward to my next respite break, which would once again see me heading back to the Sunshine Coast. This time, I had timed it so that Jen's daughter, who I used to babysit, would be giving birth to her first child, and I couldn't wait to see the family again and share such a special moment.

About a month before my holiday, I received a phone call out of the blue, and within moments of answering, I recognised a voice that I hadn't heard from for years. It was from Luke. Nearly six years had flown by since I had last seen or spoken to him, and the last words we said to each other ended a friendship that had spanned over fifteen years. It was as though we hadn't missed a beat and we instantly settled into our old banter and spent a good couple of hours chatting about everything that had happened during the years we hadn't remained in contact.

I told him he was an idiot, and he reiterated it back, and all was forgotten. It was a heartwarming conversation. We laughed at where life had taken us and how old we had suddenly gotten as he gushed over the new dryer he had just bought and I compared notes about the cordless vacuum that I had purchased, which was definitely not living up to its advertising pitch. I wasn't sure if I would have time to see him on my upcoming holiday back home as I would only be there for three days and had plans set in place. He was likely going to be away at an event. But it was comforting to be in touch, and we promised to keep each other in the loop of any exciting adventures occurring in our lives.

In the month leading up to my trip, I focused so hard on working on myself, hoping there was something I could improve to bring the magic back in my marriage, but I was starting to feel alone. I don't think there is a worse emotion of feeling alone when you are surrounded by people, certainly people who love you. I loved Ben deeply too, but something had changed, and we grew apart. We were soon more like best friends who shared a house. We would laugh and at times disagree, but we'd settled into what felt like a silent agreement of accepting that things were no longer what they once were.

We spoke about seeking couples therapy now and then during that year, but as our relationship wasn't in any way tumultuous, we sort of let it slide. It wasn't uncomfortable so much as we both recognised what was happening and just allowed it to be so. Deep in my heart though, I felt sadness, that no matter how wonderful and caring someone was, I was perhaps just destined never to experience that real true love and find the ultimate soulmate. It was a dream I had held dear since I was young, and as I approached my thirtieth birthday, I thought that maybe this was the best it was going to be. In reality, it wasn't at all horrible. Ben and I got along great, but ours was not romantic, passionate love, more a platonic love and respect.

The prior few years had seen us deal with more heartache, stress, and grief than anyone should have to face, and we had steadfastly stood united during every step. But that old me had changed, and it didn't matter what part I worked on—the relationship didn't fit for me anymore. There had been some actions by Ben that had caused me some deep hurt and made me develop some trust issues in the relationship during some pivotal moments in the past, but it wasn't the catalyst for our change in devotion.

Our struggles were kept a secret from our family and friends as we desperately tried to continue with daily life, truly both hoping something would change. We didn't want any more sadness in our lives, so we pretended as best we could—to each other and ourselves—that it was going to be okay. Deep down in my heart, I knew it wasn't, and my soul ached for what had been. As I packed my bag for my weekend away in Queensland, I hoped the few days apart would offer some clarity on what we could do next.

I had organised a bus transfer from the airport to my hotel, and a couple of days before leaving, I received a message from Luke, who explained that his event was no longer happening. He said that as I already had plans with friends and not a lot of downtime booked in for the short couple of days I was there, he would like to at least pick me up from the airport to finally catch up after all those years of not being in touch. I wasn't too sure, though. I had imagined delving into a book and a glass of wine the moment I stepped off the plane. So, I kept my transfer in place and was rather nonchalant in my response to Luke's offer. Jen's daughter Kate gave birth two days before my arrival and the thought of snuggling her son, who instantly felt like the extended family I had always dreamed of, had me on a high. This time, as the plane took off back towards my hometown, I was elated and felt that—for the first time in so long—I was heading somewhere I belonged. I had roots there, and this made me feel less adrift in a world that had overwhelmed me time and time again.

I was heading back for the second time, not needing saving, not needing validation or anything other than to breathe in the salt air that instantly took me back to more innocent times in my childhood. I could not wait. I remember the feeling of weight being lifted from my chest as my plane taxied down the runway; I knew I would be able to leave the confused state of my marriage and my sleepless nights for a weekend, and that was enough to bring calm to my soul instantly. I had no idea that once again, my life was about to take a different path the moment my plane landed at the Sunshine Coast Airport. There was absolutely nothing that could have hinted to what was about to unfold. My now well-tuned sixth sense had abandoned me, and I didn't have a clue about what awaited me at the other end.

CHAPTER 13

BURN YOUR NAME

It goes without saying that right when you least expect something to happen, that's usually when it will. When I stepped off the plane at the Sunshine Coast and collected my bag to head to the bus transfer depot, I felt my lungs fill up with the salt air of home, and I grinned, feeling instantly back where I belonged. I pulled my small suitcase behind me and made my way to the exit doors. Standing against a pole with his arms crossed and sunglasses over his eyes was an old friend that I hadn't seen in six years.

I had changed a lot in that time, and my blonde hair sat curled around my now–heavily tattooed shoulders and arms. My black leather pants, bold red lipstick, and a confident grin were a world away from the broken girl who last slammed the phone down on him all those years ago. I had known Luke for nearly two decades, and through everything we had shared I had never seen him lost for words. He stood frozen in place. I, too, momentarily stopped short as soon as I recognised him, before breaking into a fast dash in his direction. The moment I got close and wrapped my arms around my long-lost friend, he broke and his voice cracked as he hugged me close to his chest.

I told him I still had my transfer bus organised, he called me the same stubborn girl he had known forever, and we laughed as he grabbed my bag and headed towards his car in the parking lot. I can't even start to explain what happened over the next seventy-two hours; I just knew that I instantly found what I had been missing all those years. They say true love needs a combination of timing and fate to be fulfilled, and all at once it fell together. But for that to happen, everything I had built had to be pulled apart.

It was as though not a second had passed without us being in contact and those few years where our stubborn and hurt souls refused to back down and let each other back in disappeared the moment we saw each other again. The timing had never been right. I mean, I was living in a different state, married to someone else, and had two children. But the timing for us had arrived.

I had never been so sure of something in my life. The first night, as we talked until the sun came up, I knew instantly that everything was about to change. All those years, all that back and forth, all the wrong timing—that was all finished, and our time to finally be together was now.

We laughed as he pulled out a hidden box that he had kept for all those years that featured all the letters that we passed back and forth from high school, birthday cards I had sent over the years, and every photo that I had ever given him of myself and Rhyz. In all the years between us, he had never removed the ring I had given him, and he waited patiently with a treasure trove of love letters while time finally turned in our favour and I would come home to him.

I didn't know how the future would play out, but I *did* know that my heart belonged with Luke and his with mine. It had always been there; it had never gone away, and all it took was one look, and we knew. We spent those three days with our friends, Sam, Trina, my adopted mum, Jen, who had known Luke since we were twelve-year-old kids, Kate, and her gorgeous new son. We laughed and drank and stayed up until dawn every morning, sharing all the moments we had missed together over the years.

The night before I was due to go home, I told Luke I had to leave my husband. I wanted no response from him, no expectations, or any thoughts of a relationship, but I had feelings for him, and they were too strong and too lasting to be going anywhere. I couldn't possibly live with myself for lying to Ben about something like this.

I said it so matter-of-factly that it truly didn't matter if I could never be with Luke; if I was to be alone then at least I was not lying to my husband about where my heart lay. To stay and know someone held a piece of my soul to such a degree would not only be disloyal, but it would mean Ben would never have the chance of finding his true love who could give him the full devotion he deserved.

Luke looked me directly in my eyes and said, 'I love you, and I always have.' And that was it. I knew what I had to do next. We sobbed the whole way to the airport. When he had to drop me at the departure lounge, I could barely walk onto the plane without my chest heaving as I refused to look back at the terminal. Luke, meanwhile, had to pull his truck over to the side of the road once he left the airport as he couldn't see through the tears. We had no idea of what was going to happen; all we knew was that we were not going to let another moment go by with life keeping us apart.

I stepped off the plane at about 5 pm to my wonderful family waiting for me with open arms. I managed to make it through dinner and put all the children to bed and told Ben I needed to talk to him.

We stepped outside, and I opened up to him. 'I am really sorry,' I began. 'I know we have been spending a long time trying to work through our relationship issues, but I can't do it any longer. I have feelings for someone who I gave my heart to many years ago, and I want to separate.'

I explained that I didn't know what I was going to do next, just that I knew my heart belonged with someone else. I was willing to take whatever anger, frustration, and pain was duly deserved, but I just needed to tell him straight away.

'Are you certain?' he asked through tears, and I nodded through my sadness, and we knew it was over.

'I don't know what will happen next, but, Ben, I just want to go home now. It's been so long, and I know you don't want to come with me, but even if we are separated, I would love to have us all move up there. We could co-parent up there, and I am ready to take my children home.'

Ben shook his head and said that, like me, he was finally home where he grew up, and he didn't want to leave again. I understood, but we kept the option open and decided to talk about what we would do next in the coming weeks while we adjusted to the new situation.

We both knew it was coming. Behind the façade we put up for family and friends, we had been struggling for quite some time. Not in a nasty, bitter, or argumentative way, but a slow realisation while we were on our journey as parents to a medically complex child. We did try during those early years; we knew deep down that we were great friends, but the love wasn't the same, and both of us were missing something. He just wasn't my soulmate or my true love, and I wasn't his, and nothing could change that.

He left home the very next day and then we went to couples counselling for a few weeks, which I think helped him understand it wasn't anything he did wrong or could change about himself. He was perfect the way he was, but perfect for someone else, and I was the same. My heart belonged elsewhere, and for the first time in decades, I was about to finally let my heart be open to the person who I gave my heart and soul to at fourteen years old.

My gym friends were quite vocal about my decision to leave my husband, and instead of even asking me what had happened, I was subjected to vile messages and humiliating reactions when I would see them in public. Suddenly the small town I had tried to make a home in was growing smaller by the minute, and I was a marked woman. None of this changed the way I knew I felt. If I had to live alone in a small town that made me feel like a pariah, then that was the price I was willing to pay to feel I was living a life I had chosen finally.

I felt so strongly about my decision. I was confident that if nothing ever happened with my relationship with Luke, then I was, for the first time in ages, taking a risk that although was entirely selfish, would have me living with peace within myself. I just couldn't stay feeling like I couldn't breathe any longer.

The hardest part was explaining to Rhyz that it was all my final decision that Ben and I were separating. I wanted to be genuinely open and honest with him so that he didn't feel as though anything was untoward or that we were hiding anything from him. I explained to him that I had feelings for someone else, and I was truly sorry for this. As a teenage boy, he was confused, but also understood that things had been at times stressful between his dad and me. I consoled him the best I could with the knowledge that Ben would always be his father, and that he would (as would all his family members) remain a permanent figure and role model in his life. While I wasn't sure how this would all play out, it would be done respectfully and as stress-free and straightforward as possible.

It wasn't easy initially while we all found our feet with this new arrangement, but the children came first, and they were able to spend as much time as they wanted at either house. They quickly realised there was no nastiness or bitterness between us, although the sadness was obviously there for both of us. What I wanted to accomplish more than anything was to ensure my children were never subjected to the same issues I dealt with as a teenager when my parents separated. Ben and I took the high road and refused to ever have the children feel uncomfortable in our presence or about what was happening. The transition was easier than expected; Ben and I resumed our friendship, we just didn't live in the same house anymore. It was different, but it was certainly stress-free for the children, and I will always be so proud of how we handled ourselves during our separation.

Luke and I spoke almost nightly at this point, and I wondered where the next step was going to take me. Within a few days, I had decided to move back to the Sunshine Coast—my home—as I had always wanted. The doctors and specialists had already recommended this move many times to assist Corbin's lung disease, and I knew they had no problem transferring his care to another region. Most of his major surgeries had been completed, with only a couple more needing to be carried out in Melbourne by a specialist surgeon.

There was a fantastic liver transplant team in the Queensland Children's Hospital in Brisbane and paediatric surgeons and specialists that could take over from Melbourne's care. Even though I kept encouraging Ben to move too so that we could both share parenting easily up there, he didn't want to move from his hometown, and I understood. He had spent the previous ten years of his life travelling the world and Australia until we met in Fremantle. He just wanted to be home now, too.

With the biggest heart that anyone has ever shown me, he agreed I could move back to the Sunshine Coast with our boys, and we set about making an agreement that would work the best for our family's unique situation. The first part was we were not going to have any child support involved. I would cover all the day-to-day living expenses and costs for medications and schooling, sports, etc. and Ben would keep the private health cover for Corbin and cover his airfares for any visits. We would work as a team to always make sure the boys got everything they needed without either of us having to go broke to provide for them. I could always ask for financial help if I needed it, and I have. One day the health insurance card didn't work at a rather expensive dental appointment for Corbin, and I didn't have enough money to cover it. A quick phone call and Ben settled the account within minutes. Once you take money out of the equation, there is a lot less stress, and the focus can purely be on the children.

We left a joint bank account open where, to this day, we place money for extra things for the children, and it works brilliantly. There was also a stipulation Ben would be able to video call every day, and I can honestly say that in the past eight years, I doubt he has missed more than seven days. Those times were usually due to something simple like one of us falling asleep early or having a phone issue.

Once it was agreed my time had come to move home, it was all systems go. Luke, who had been supportive of any decision I made from the very beginning, was beside himself with excitement. Within a few days of the agreement being sorted, he had booked himself a surprise plane ticket and turned up on my doorstep for a fly-in fly-out twenty-four-hour hug. He also got to meet Rhyz again, and tiny Corbin was introduced to him for the first time. It was incredibly exciting, and I was nervous that Luke might be a little overwhelmed with Corbin's medical condition. At that stage, he was being 90% fed via his stomach tube but had succeeded in eating real food. Well, not 'eating' as such, but he would chew the food and then spit it into another bowl beside the main plate. It was somewhat off-putting, but vital for him so as to not develop a total aversion to eating altogether.

Luke didn't bat an eyelid, and the boys swarmed around him as though they instantly connected. It was heartwarming to watch. We had decided the move was going to be best done after Christmas so that Rhyz could start at his new high school at the beginning of the year. This only left about ten weeks to get everything organised. We had decided that once we left, Ben would move back into the house we had together, which made it easy for everyone. In the meantime, I started to pack some boxes and organise for new furniture to be purchased.

Ben and I decided to split the furniture equally, so each person only had to buy a few things each to make a full house again. It helped keep both houses familiar for the children as well. I ordered new beds, mattresses, dining table, and lounges in advance, so it was all ready to collect at the other end.

I started to panic about six weeks before the move, hoping I was making the right choice, and wondering if moving home was going to be everything I had spent years dreaming it would be. *Was I really going to have my fairytale ending?* Luke had been incredibly supportive of me, but I was so painfully stubborn in not wanting to appear fragile that I refused to lean on him for help. I can recall having twenty-four hours of just crying and being so worried if I was doing the right thing, if being selfish for the first time was going to undo all the hard work I had done building up a family and a place to call home for my sons. On the evening of my day of panic, who else pulls up my driveway after driving for two solid days but Luke? It must have been a case of instinctively knowing I needed him; he had known me for almost two decades at this stage, and he already had a plan well underway.

I stood shell-shocked as he explained that he had taken his long service leave, had his tools in the back of his truck and job interviews lined up, and even a room to stay in if we felt that it was too soon for him to stay with us. But he insisted he wasn't returning home without me.

'I haven't waited seventeen years to lose you now, and I will stay as long as it takes to bring you home.'

I cried on his shoulder as I realised the lengths he had gone to in order to be there and all those times he had tried to step in and be a family with me for so long. I knew then it was all going to be okay.

And sure enough, in mid-January, we watched as a removalist truck carried our belongings back to my hometown, and I got on a plane with Rhyz and Corbin to meet Luke. He had taken the drive home earlier that week so he could meet us at the airport.

By this stage, he had organised for his entire house to be fitted out with all the new furniture I had bought. It was transformed from a bachelor pad—featuring car parts in spare rooms and the lack of an essential dining table—into a perfect family home with every room filled with toys, books, and even a gaming room for Rhyz.

We had finally arrived home—a new blended family in a town where I belonged and that would now belong to my children too. Ben and his mum and dad came to visit within the first few months, and then, of course, the regular holidays with the boys began back and forth. It went seamlessly. There was a lot of mutual respect, communication, and making sure, as much as possible, that no-one felt excluded. Special holidays such as Christmas, Easter, and the school holidays were all for Corbin and Rhyz to spend with their dad and his family.

I still have had no problem with that; I get the luxury of seeing them every day. We simply celebrate prior to or after those special days. If the parent is missing out on, for example, a birthday or Mother's day or Father's day then the other parent always goes that extra mile with presents and video calls to make sure there is still that feeling of being irreplaceable. It is always about going that extra mile, in every area of life; when there are children involved, it is paramount.

And so, finally, after so many years of feeling like I wasn't sure of my place in the world, I knew exactly where I belonged: home again with my high school sweetheart—my first love and my true love—and my family.

CHAPTER 14

THIS OLD LOVE

I can recall precisely where I was standing when I had one of my very first conversations with Luke about children. I was a couple of champagnes in and calmly asked him if he would be quite content to live happily with the family we had or was having children an important dream of his. I asked this expecting a somewhat different response to the one I received. After all, he was past thirty years old, I already had two sons, and we were the typical nuclear, blended family of four.

He looked at me as though I had suddenly asked him to run away and join a circus with me and said, incredibly seriously, 'Oh no, I want a big family, at least two more children. Oh, I would like us to be married as well.' I can remember needing to take a seat on his old, wooden veranda at this stage. I waited for him to laugh, but he didn't; he was deadly serious. I remember making mention of the fact that not only had I been a mother since I was sixteen years old, but Corbin's care needs were quite overwhelming at times, and that more children really wasn't in my plan.

I was rather tired, and the thought of having another child was quite shocking. I had sort of presumed we would just stay in our lovely little bubble, and I guess he had presumed we were about to expand that bubble, and considerably.

I wasn't too sure how I felt about marriage either. After all, I was in the midst of finalising my divorce from my third husband, and I had not yet celebrated my thirty-first birthday. I don't think being married was my strong suit. I obviously was great at being proposed to and getting married, but making it stick—that's when it all went a little wonky donkey.

I soon realised just how important having children was to Luke. He had always imagined himself as a father. I knew due to our age— being over thirty—we didn't have much time to dillydally over the subject, and I did very much want to grow our family. I think the option had just never crossed my mind.

Then, before we knew it, we had yet another brother on his way to join our family. I was thrilled when it was confirmed that we would have a child together, and Luke—well, he just turned to instant mush and became such a sentimental soul. He was walking on cloud nine and bulletproof. Luke cried at the first ultrasound and carried the sonogram print with him everywhere he went. He was overcome with happiness and was so proud he could barely contain himself.

Luke was such a nostalgic sweetheart that when I moved in, he pulled out an old cardboard box—that smelled of old socks—from under all the hats he had stored (hence the smell, I believe). He had kept, for nearly two decades, the letters I had written him back in high school, the special occasion cards I had sent over the years, and even the wrapping paper and gift box that held the fifteenth birthday present I gave him. Luke was so sentimental and had waited for his fairytale ending, and I was so blessed that it included me. I had never had anyone love me so sincerely as he did before and to this day; I am the most grateful and luckiest person in the world to be with my soulmate.

On my birthday that year, he presented me with a jewellery box that looked strangely familiar. It belonged to a jeweller that used to have a business at the local shopping centre when we were teenagers.

Luke had managed to track down and order the same forget-me-not-ring from the same jeweller he had purchased the first from nearly two decades earlier. I was touched that he went to such lengths. The jeweller said that he remembered him coming in all those years ago as a teenager, and he recounted the story of how Luke had sold his skates at a second-hand store to buy the ring initially, and although the gentleman was closing the business, he was honoured to remake the ring for such a special purpose.

Then, to add to the celebrations, he decided to take me out on a date night on his boat, which was incredible and nostalgic. He drove us over to Bribie Island, where we used to play when we were teenagers in love. He made a delicious platter of food and set up huge tiki torches to light up the beach; it was just gorgeous. Then, right when I least expected it, he dropped to one knee, opened a box containing a stunning engagement ring, and asked me to be his wife. I instantly knew this was the fairytale I had always dreamed of, and he was the man I was going to build my life with. I didn't hesitate to say, 'Yes!'

*

Luke and I walked around grinning from ear to ear, discussing wedding plans and trying to decide on baby names; it was a wonderful time in our lives, and we felt we were living in a dream.

I was confident and certain about everything we were doing, but the pregnancy itself had me secretly scared. I hid it from Luke the entire pregnancy, but the fear nearly paralysed me. The doctors were great, knowing Corbin's condition, and, although it is not genetic, they still went above and beyond with testing and ultrasounds to ensure bub was completely healthy. While Luke would be grinning like a Cheshire cat at each appointment, I would sit with a fake smile plastered on my face, pretending to believe it wasn't going to be another experience like Corbin's birth. I knew I wouldn't believe anything until I held this baby in my arms.

Rhyz, who had experienced his own loss and devastation with the miscarriage and then with Corbin's birth, was as reserved as I was. Although this time the pregnancy went smoothly—I was healthier than I had ever been and felt fantastic during the nine months—there was still a slight niggle in my mind that never entirely went away.

I never wanted to take those special moments away from Luke, so I kept them to myself and allowed him to feel secure in our son's future, while I just prayed this time it would all be alright.

Sure enough, it was, and I delivered a very healthy baby boy who we named Dash. He was all bright blue eyes like his dad and fair-haired like us both, and the relief when they passed me my perfect pink son was overwhelming. I couldn't have been more grateful that he was perfectly healthy. Rhyz was over the moon; this was the first time he'd had a newborn baby to dote over, hold, and enjoy without worry, and he adored him. It was a beautiful time in our lives.

Rhyz was excelling so well at school he skipped a grade entirely and became one of the youngest students in his class. His brain went a mile a minute and held information brilliantly, and he would ace his tests while barely studying. In the mornings, he would do a ten-kilometre run before breakfast to keep his fitness up. Rhyz made a fantastic group of friends at school and even joined the local soccer club, where he became one of the rare players to be selected in the under-eighteen team when he was still only fourteen. Always dedicated to joining the army, Rhyz studied the classes he needed to maximise his chances to enrol when he left school.

He grew fast, seemingly overnight, and by the time he was fifteen, he was already six feet tall and a strong athletic machine. He had begged me to allow him to join the local gym, and in between his high school classes and a part-time job, he would hit the gym with his mates at night-time and became committed to pursuing his life goals.

We all couldn't cheer loudly enough for him. Rhyz had become a handsome, intelligent, and charming young man, but more importantly than that—and what matters most to me—he was kind;

his heart was filled with compassion and love. He would be the first person to assist with taking an older person's groceries to their car, and always stood up for those who have been mistreated. Rhyz was becoming a man with morals, principals, and ethics who made me proud.

I don't know if I did much right when it came to making decisions and choices on how to be a mother, but when I looked at my teenage son standing in front of me filled with well-earned self-confidence and the knowledge he is loved and can love others, then I know I must have done something right.

I will forever base my competence as a human who is worthy of respect on whether I have managed to raise children who have faith in themselves and know they are capable of anything, and this young man indeed showed every sign of that.

Being a mother to three boys filled me with a purpose and over-whelming love. I never stop counting my blessings. Their happiness is directly linked to mine, and I live to watch them smile and hear their laughter fill my house.

Corbin's lungs had undoubtedly taken a liking to the warmer weather, and I shall never forget the day my little boy saw the ocean for the first time. It was as though a magnet was pulling him. He squealed with laughter as his toes touched the sand at Kings Beach for the first time, the same place I used to spend my summers growing up, and then at top speed he took off running towards the waves. He has been an ocean soul from the very beginning, and it has been a magnificent benefit to his health in so many ways.

Luke and I, with our growing family, soon realised we were going to need an extra income to support us. Luke had an investment property and a rather expensive weekly mortgage on the home we lived in, and then there were repayments needed to cover his toys: boats, car builds, motorbikes, etc. All of this was easy for him to maintain when he had roommates in his bachelor pad who paid board, but then the family life came about, and it all started to get rather tight.

We decided I was going to have to go back to work. We would have to find a private nanny or nurse who could look after both Corbin and Dash a couple of days a week, and I would need to find a dental nursing position that would allow me to work around Corbin's special appointments, which he still attended every couple of weeks to have the portacath in his chest flushed.

I found the perfect nanny who was trained in every area we needed and set about finding a place I would like to work. I printed out my resume with a cover letter explaining my unique situation. I hoped like heck a dentist would even accept the fact I was already asking for regular time off before I even started.

I looked in my local area and found an impressive orthodontic practice called Invisible Orthodontics. Their website boasted orthodontic specialist care, paediatric dentistry, general dentistry, and a highly professional team. It was led by a highly respected orthodontist named Vas Srinivasan. I thought to myself, *Well, you may as well shoot for the stars here and give it your all; there is nothing left to lose.* I made a call and asked if I could come in and have an appointment with the doctor. They weren't advertising a vacant position, but they had a brilliant professional reputation, and I wanted to work beside such highly commendable specialists.

By this stage, Dash was three months old. The rates notices had come for the two properties, along with a few extra medical expenses due to a recent surgery Corbin had in Melbourne after we arrived back on the coast. We knew we would be struggling to buy groceries the following fortnight, let alone pay all the bills that were mounting up.

I walked into the practice nervous but hopeful. Luke had driven me there, and he and the three kids sat in the car, waiting for me around the corner where they couldn't be seen. Ushered into my interview, I explained my situation to the doctor with the kind eyes. I could only start after 9 am as I needed to run my son's last tube feed, but I promised to work hard and become a dedicated and valued team member. I explained that sometimes I would need to take time off to be with my son in the hospital. I was sure he would say 'no'. I looked to be more a liability than an asset. I had a great resume, but now I had other serious priorities I could not change.

He reached across the table, shook my hand, and asked if I could start the next week. I just about fell over. He said they would work around anything I needed; it was no bother, and the pay grade that I asked for (which was considerably higher than anything I had received before) was accepted on the spot! I was told if I met the regular position assessments, there would not only be pay rises but plenty of further training opportunities as well.

I think I levitated out of the office. I still don't know if that man knows what he did for us that day. He gave me a role that was more than just being a mother to a medically complex child, which for the past few years had taken over quite a bit of my identity. It is hard to explain, but being able to be 'normal' for a few hours a week at work was just something I never dreamed of having the privilege of doing again. There were yelps of excitement when I got back in the car! We knew we would make it; all it was going to take was hard work, dedication, and love.

The love part we had in bucketloads, and every day we grinned at each other over the dinner table and felt like we were the luckiest people in the world to have each other.

We decided to marry on an extravagant island in the Whitsundays in Queensland, in a glass chapel overlooking the ocean at night, with candles and roses to fill the pews. We were not going to tell anyone about our elopement. We had the perfect plan. As the budget was tight, we knew we couldn't afford a big wedding, but we could afford this beautiful elopement package that allowed us to stay on a tropical island for a couple of days as we drank cocktails in swim-up bars, kayaked beside gigantic turtles, and shared the most romantic and beautiful wedding ceremony in our dream location.

I walked down the aisle to the same song Luke played for me all those years before when we were only fourteen years old and he had filled my teenage bedroom with roses. I held the same brilliantly red roses studded with cascading diamantes, and my heart soared as I walked toward the man who had loved and waited for me for nearly two decades. He had tears rolling down his face as we said our vows, and we danced and drank champagne and toasted to our future together and all the dreams we had. I felt like I was the luckiest person in the world: I was marrying my best friend, a man who I could not only laugh and cry with, but who made me feel like he was my 'home'.

We then returned home, and two days later, under the guise of our engagement party at a hugely popular restaurant called Rick's Diner, we pulled up right out the front in a Chevy® decorated with white ribbons. I stepped out of the wedding car carrying my wedding bouquet, to the surprise and excitement of all our friends and family. We partied till they closed, drank the bar dry of Patron®, and had the time of our lives. The wedding photos taken by a professional on the island were played on the big televisions around the room as the jukebox cranked out tunes. It was everything we ever wanted and more. A couple of weeks later, we discovered the best wedding present of all; I was pregnant again with our youngest son. This time, there was no panic. As a family, we celebrated wholeheartedly, dreaming of the brilliant year we were about to have ahead of us.

Rhyz was killing it at school, and Corbin's health was stable; he had only needed one lung-related ambulance trip to hospital in the two years we had been on the coast. He had undergone quite a few surgical procedures and planned operations, but his organs were holding up wonderfully. Dash was a big bundle of smiles, and I had a job that was helping us keep it all together. It was February 2015 when we had confirmation that our newest and last addition to our family was to be another son, and we collectively felt this year was about to be wonderful. Oh, how very wrong we were.

CHAPTER 15

SUGAR, WE'RE GOING DOWN SWINGING

We felt like 2015 had the potential to be the most victorious year of our lives. However, it was the year that will go down in history as the worst our family had ever experienced. The year started on such a high note, having just celebrated our wedding and the announcement of our pregnancy. But what began as a slow-moving avalanche soon picked up speed until we were shells of our former selves, with nothing left but each other and pure faith that we could put the pieces of our broken lives back together.

I went straight back to work after our wedding in January, and it was planned that I would work through until August, just a few weeks before our son was due, so we would all stay afloat financially. We set about putting a few plans into motion to fulfil our next stage in life.

One of those big ideas was to sell Luke's investment property and use the profits from that to make the necessary renovations to bring the house we were living in up to the correct codes and modernise it as much as possible. Then we would sell that and use the profits to buy a lovely old Queenslander on a big block of land, where the children would be able to grow up and roam and have the country-style upbringing we dreamed of giving them.

We had a book that we kept—like a scrapbook, I guess. We would keep cut-outs of ideas of what we could do to this new house of ours. We would talk about how we would fill it with antique furniture and record players, and the children would be able to bring their children there every Sunday to share a family roast. It was going to be our little slice of heaven and our family legacy, where all our boys would build memories and future generations would too. We were so excited; we knew to make this happen; we just had to keep working and pushing ahead.

All of this was feasible. I had job security; I was able to take as little or as much maternity leave as I wanted, and Luke's senior role as a director in his family business was, of course, guaranteed. So long as we kept steering the boat in the right direction, we would be bound to see the year out with our dreams unfolding. There is a saying that when you are in a lifeboat, make sure everyone is paddling in the same direction, and no-one is drilling holes when you aren't looking.

Sadly, for us, holes were being drilled everywhere around us, and before we knew it, we were going under fast. Our first mistake came when we put the investment property on the market. To do this, we got a small loan so that we could freshen up the carpets and paint and complete a few touch-ups. That was not a concern as we knew there was such good equity in the house itself that when it sold, it would not only pay off that small loan, but it would cover the extensive renovations needed for our current family home for us to put it on the market.

At that stage, it was a well-thought-out plan: a little more debt now would, in turn, allow us to make all the other loans go away. We would be left with a family home that the bank and real estate agent had recently valued in the low-to-mid $600,000 region. Our calculations gave us a reasonable $150,000-$200,000 to use as a deposit on our dream Queenslander late in the year and also to have us completely debt-free. With the personal loan that I had taken out to move to Queensland and two credit cards I had extended to their utmost limit to cover Corbin's medical, nutritional milk for his tube feeds, medications, and travel expenses to his hospital appointments in both Brisbane and Melbourne, we were financially pushing uphill. We kept positive and knew the light would soon be visible once these next few months passed.

We were going alright, and with the $20,000 loan we had taken out for the investment property renovations, we had a little remaining. Just before we put the house on the market, Luke took me down to a house we drove by on our family Sunday cruises, where a black Ford XP Falcon® had sat with long grass growing around it for as long as we could remember. He made a deal with the young surfer who opened the door, and before I knew it, Luke had bought me my first dream car that we would work together to rebuild in our garage.

It didn't run properly; it needed a lot of work, but it was thrilling. I had always had a passion for classic cars, and to be able to do one up was going to be a family affair. Luke was a diesel mechanic by trade and working on the mechanical side was going to be a walk in the park for him.

We used to sit in the back seat of this broken-down XP in the garage, and the kids would sit in the front pretending to drive. We would tell them how this was going to be the family car that, just like the new house we were on our way to getting, would be part of their history.

It was such a romantic notion, and if only I could go back in time and sit us both down and slap us into the reality of what was to come, I would. But sadly, I don't think it would make a difference to what happened next. The investment property went on the market in February and sold within two weeks. Our excitement was raised to the next level when we realised it sold for the asking price, which would leave us $50,000 after all expenses. That would easily cover the $20,000 we had borrowed and the $30,000 we expected to need to cover the renovations for the family home. We were ecstatic and just waited for the money to hit our account so we could start booking in the professionals to make changes to our home.

Just to keep us on our toes, my pregnancy this time round was horrible. Our son had managed to get himself stuck in a strange spot as he grew, pressing on a nerve that ran down my back and my leg, which left me wrapped up in support bands under my nursing scrubs. The pain was excruciating, and the doctors had prescribed me the painkiller oxycodone from five months to even be able to stand up.

I was told I needed to be on bed rest, but sadly that would have left us short financially and unable to meet the debt we had accrued. I also had developed a nice waddle early on to compensate for the pain, and it was quite funny to watch. My stomach had popped quite early on, due to this being baby number four, and I was less than graceful and struggled to move around the patients' heads at work. My understanding boss moved me out to the reception area and also created a new position involving steri nursing (sterilising all the instruments), stocktake, and data entry, which kept me off my swelling ankles. I could not be more grateful for working with such a fantastic team.

The nurses who worked beside me—Mandy, Bianca, and Viv— knew how much pain I was in daily. They understood I needed to keep working to put food on the table; our debts were too high, and we didn't qualify for any government assistance due to our assets and Luke's pay grade. They helped me keep my pain and inability to move well a secret from our boss, as we knew he would have sent me home to rest out of concern for my wellbeing. But I had used all my holidays, carer's leave, and sick leave on my son's medical appointments, and to be eligible for the twelve weeks of maternity leave I had to work up until two weeks before my due date.

These beautiful friends hold a special place in my heart as they would help hold me upright as they snuck me upstairs on lunch breaks and they would set the alarm and come and wake me up and help me back downstairs again where no-one would be any the wiser. They helped keep up the joke that it was easier to wheel me around in a nurse's chair so the senior dentists and our boss never realised I couldn't stand that day.

I had to wait each day until I got to work to take the painkillers as you cannot drive on them. Because they made me nauseous, I had to wash them down with anti-nausea tablets to make them bearable. I was no longer nursing with patients at all, but if I was asked to step in and help, without a breath, another nurse from the team would instantly jump up and say she wanted to assist with the patient. It meant I never had to explain why I couldn't help as it was morally and legally wrong for me to assist while using such strong pain killers. These wonderful women also allowed me to save face, and I would carry on with my data entry as though nothing was wrong. After work, Bianca would even drive my car to the front door once our boss had left, as I couldn't quite walk far enough without needing assistance. They were the kindest and most caring people I had ever met.

One day I was at work at the front reception beside Mandy and I attempted to pull myself forward on my wheeled office chair to be closer to the desk. Clearly, I was too front-heavy, and within seconds, I found myself landing quite suddenly and firmly on my bottom. My chair had flung backwards, hitting the wall and the fan at the same time, making quite a racket and leaving the patients in reception wondering what happened to the blonde head that had just been making small talk to them above the desk.

Mandy and Bianca came running. After they realised it was only my pride that was hurt, it soon turned into a comedy routine. That escalated as we realised I had managed to lose a shoe on the way down. I mean, seriously, it was a tie-on nursing shoe around a fat swollen foot; I have no idea how it came off. Then, because I was stuck on the ground with this enormous stomach, it was a rather small space to try to get a pregnant woman back off the ground. They tried pulling me up, but I couldn't exactly bend in the middle, so then it was decided they would roll me on to all fours and help me regain my footing from there. By now, I was in fits of laughter; my face was beet-red from embarrassment, but I was laughing so hard at the absolute ridiculousness of the whole scenario that I could barely catch my breath.

Now the patients waiting in reception had started to get the giggles, and once my fellow employees finally managed to get me to my feet, there was laughter everywhere. I took my shoe that had come off in one hand and hobbled back to a spare surgery where I needed my friend Bianca to tie my shoe back on as I couldn't reach down there anymore. It was the funniest moment of my pregnancy and had us giggling for a long time.

*

The money from the sale of the investment property was taking its time coming into the bank, and Luke called them regularly to ask what was going on. Each time, he was assured it would be another day or two, and we were getting a little nervous. It had been a month now and no money, only the same response. So, Luke ended up going down there in person and requesting to speak to the manager. The moment he walked back in the door with his face ashen, I knew something had gone wrong. The easiest way he could explain it to me was that the person at the bank who he had been dealing with was a new staff member without much training.

The bank manager had to explain to my husband that due to the investment property being used initially as collateral for him to finance the family home, it meant all the profits from the sale instantly went into the family home mortgage, without the ability to redraw on them. The new staff member had repeatedly confirmed this was not going to be the case due to the large amount of equity that we had built up in the family home. So in short, while the investment property had sold and the mortgage of the family home had a large chunk paid off it, we still had the $20,000 debt from the renovation loan and absolutely no money to bring the family home up to the standard needed to sell. Essentially, we had just acquired more debt and were further away from where we originally began. It was a tough blow, and it took a bit for us to get our head around how we would get out of this hole of debt we seemed to be digging deeper.

It was roughly at this point that Luke's family business decided to do some 'restructuring'. There were five people in the family business: two parents and the three brothers, all directors and equal shareholders. The directors voted for Luke to be removed from his senior position and put him back on the tools, to make the business more efficient. Then it was voted that he would be working at least an hour's drive away at job sites regularly. I, therefore, needed to switch my work hours to accommodate his long drive home; I had to finish early to relieve Corbin's carer instead of Luke doing this, and we started to lose money very quickly.

By the end of June, he no longer had a company car as it was given back to the family company. He was also now being sent over to Fraser Island for a couple of days at a time for work, leaving me to manage three children, a job, and a painful pregnancy that left me barely able to walk. Without the ability for me to continue to keep the current work hours I had, we couldn't meet our debt repayments no matter how hard we worked.

We knew this was just the start; you know that feeling you get when you can sense that something awful is about to happen? That tightening of the chest, like just before the roller coaster reaches its peak and starts its descent? That is where we were, and it was petrifying.

On my birthday that year, I stood in the driveway and watched as my XP was taken away to its new owner's house so we could afford to meet our mortgage repayments that month. Not long after that, we reached rock bottom when our bank card was declined at the grocery store. It was humiliating. I was at home with Corbin that day, nursing him through another rough medical moment, when Luke came through the front door holding Dash and, with tears in his eyes, looking utterly defeated. He explained how he had called people for help, but he had been turned away. I had never seen him so broken. To have reached out for the first time in his life for help to feed his family and be denied was a humiliatingly low moment.

Just as bad timing has it, Corbin's portacath popped out under his collarbone during a routine flush. It didn't break through the skin, but it was obviously broken as we watched him scream in pain in my lap as the pressure in his vein made it protrude abnormally just below his neck as the nurse pushed the syringe into his port in his chest. It was hard to hold my emotions together as I tried to reassure this scared and pained little boy in my arms that it was going to be okay as I demanded the nurse stop the procedure immediately and remove the needle that was attempting to flush the port. It failed again after its replacement a few months later, so it was decided to remove it permanently. He was almost five years old at this stage, and all his organs had been running pretty stable for a while; we could maintain blood tests during routine surgeries when he was unconscious, and other medication could be placed through his stomach tube. So, in the middle of all of this, there was another surgery that we hadn't expected. But, as Corbin does, he took it in his stride and bounced back rather swiftly.

They say when you hit rock bottom, you can't fall any further. But let me tell you, being dragged along rock bottom is possibly worse, and it hurts like hell. We would lay in bed at night unable to talk, holding hands in the darkness and staring at the ceiling, not knowing how we were going to eat each week. It was, without a doubt, the lowest point we had ever seen.

Luke felt betrayed and, at that point, almost suicidal. I tried to keep his spirits up and encourage him as much as I could; I took on the extra workload at home as much as I was physically able to and continued to reassure him that we would make it through this together. It pained me to see him in such a state of heartbreak, and we would just hold each other and remind ourselves that the blessings we did have couldn't be taken away, like our beautiful family and our love.

Financially though, since the upheaval of the restructure, we were in freefall, and we just kept falling. To be a parent and in charge of providing food and shelter, and then to somehow start having it all slide away, is the worst feeling to face. We kept telling each other that we were going to be okay, that we would both just keep pushing and surely it would all get better. How this would happen, we had no idea. We were in a mountain of debt, the mortgage repayments were starting to slip, loan repayments were being missed, and debt collectors with summons would knock at the door. We hid it from the kids as best we could, and we tried to keep our heads up as much as we could and see the positives. We just knew if we had each other, then we would never give up.

Then they discovered I would need a caesarean section as our son had gotten himself stuck in the breech position and had dropped a foot down, which made for a very unpleasant last couple of weeks of pregnancy. The doctors were also concerned by the amount of blood flow to his brain; apparently, it was too much. So, they needed us to come back and check the following week. Each ultrasound was another couple of hundred dollars we didn't have and added to our credit card debts. The next week, they were concerned his femurs were too short, and we were booked in again for seven days. At the last ultrasound they said he was measuring small for his due date and pushed his delivery to be done precisely at thirty-eight weeks in case there were issues.

So, on top of the fact we were broke, emotionally destroyed, and financially losing in every avenue, we now had to wait and see if our little boy would be healthy. I had to tell my boss at this stage, and he was wonderfully supportive, allowing me to adjust my role at work to support my condition.

With Luke working long hours away from home, the pressure on us was immense, and the hospital was now giving me steroids to strengthen my son's lungs in preparation for delivery. I struggled not having my husband by my side during this due to his work placement, especially for Corbin's regular medical procedures.

Instead, I would call him sobbing after I had held Corbin down, Dash strapped in a pram beside me, and my stomach hugely pregnant, as this scared little boy would scream until he vomited and would wet himself from the fear of all the needles and the tubes that would draw blood from his chest. It was pure torture.

I was so lucky to have Jen play such an active role in our lives from the moment I came back to Queensland. As well as being there during times of celebration, she was also there during times of need, bringing home-cooked meals and always just a phone call away whenever I needed her. She stepped up during this challenging time and assisted us with bags of clothes for the kids, and in those heavily pregnant working days, she would make sure I had dinner on my doorstep if Luke was being sent away again for work. I would have been lost without her.

The day before my planned caesarean, Luke had a random call from a finance company that must have gotten his details many moons ago when we first looked at loans for the unit renovation. They asked if he wanted to take out a line of credit. Luke thought this must have been a mistake as we were both in so much debt. Surely no-one would touch us. He told the caller he needed $30,000 to renovate the family home in order to sell it and recoup the profits. The gentleman at the end of the phone said he would do some research and see what he could do. Luke laughed and said, 'Sure,' thinking there was no way someone was going to give us another loan.

That afternoon, as I was packing my hospital bag in readiness for the birth of our son, Luke raced through the house. I remember him talking so fast I had to ask him to repeat himself. When he did, I had to sit down to take it all in. He had just been approved for a $30,000 loan, and the money would be in our bank account within twenty-four hours.

The interest rate was astronomical, but he took it, as it meant that we had a shot now—that tiny sliver of hope. We could do up the family home as soon as the money touched the bank account, and put it on the market instantly. As the real estate and the bank valuer had stated we would get $600,000, if not more, this was enough to pay off all our debts, and we would have a small deposit for a home.

We could barely believe it; it was like just before you are about to break beyond repair, you are given a lifeline. As we readied ourselves to meet our son in the morning, we knew we might be able to pull this all off after all.

It was August when our little ray of sunshine entered the world. Entirely healthy, a perfect weight, with normal length femurs and a disposition that instantly filled us with love. We named him Ace Danger, and the moment in the theatre when he was lifted above the curtain, we knew he was the perfect fulfilment of our family. The caesarean itself was quite brutal, and instead of the small scar that we expected, I was cut from one hip bone to the other. It was a week before I could manage to walk more than a few metres, but with our family complete, our happiness was almost uncontainable.

*

Only four weeks after giving birth to Ace, I was a guest speaker at a fundraising event for the hospital charity Wishlist™. This kind-hearted charity supports the local community health system and the annual Give Me 5 for Kids® appeal is an essential part of providing a variety of assistance to the most vulnerable people. I managed to walk into the event with stomach strapping hidden under my gown, some heavy pain killers, and Luke's hand in mine.

We began the home renovations instantly, and we made that $30,000 stretch as far as we could by getting in professionals to start the makeover.

With the new loan in play, I didn't have the luxury of the maternity leave that I had planned on, and when little Ace was five weeks old, I had to head back to work; just a couple of short shifts a week. My boss had organised them for when the office was unattended, which meant I could take Ace with me and still breastfeed as I sorted out ordering supplies and stocktaking. I wheeled little Ace around beside me as we went. The shifts were just enough to cover the extra repayments of the new loan. Right now, we were aware we were in well over our heads, but the moment the sale of the house went through, we would all be okay. All that hard work would be worth it; we just had to keep working together as a team.

It took us a little over six weeks, but we added new decking and railings to the broken front entrance. We laid new carpets, painted inside and out, landscaped, and brought everything up to the standard we needed to put it on the market. By this time, it was early October; Ace was around seven weeks old, and Corbin's health started to decline rapidly out of nowhere.

First, his temperature spiked well over thirty-nine degrees with no other symptoms at all. I raced him to the doctor, and while he complained that his throat hurt, there wasn't anything that seemed to be the cause of his temperatures. That was around mid-week, and by Friday, Corbin had woken during the night, crying that his throat still hurt. His temperature wasn't being controlled by paracetamol, so we returned to the doctor.

This time, I asked if it could be his liver. I said I knew it was probably stupid, but his eyes looked a little funny in colour. They checked him out physically, and as his portacath had been removed recently, the pathology staff tried to access veins to see his levels but were unsuccessful. We were sent home with the thought of it being a respiratory illness or something viral and given antibiotics.

During this time, I had been sleeping at the foot of his bed, waking up to check his temperature, administer medications, and give extra nutrition through his stomach tubes, and that Friday night was hard. I was still waiting for the antibiotics to kick in and praying, as I had this terrible feeling that the doctors were wrong. Saturday came, and his temperature skyrocketed to 39.4 °C and his feet turned purple. I called an ambulance.

We made it to the local hospital, where they managed to stabilise him. After what seemed like forever, they managed to access a vein and get a line in. I sat on that theatre resuscitation table all alone for hours trying to calm a very distressed and seriously unwell little boy, as my husband remained with our three other children at home waiting on a relative to come and take over so he could join me.

The most fantastic team of doctors and nurses quickly sized up the situation as I handed over the giant colour-coded folder that held every piece of information relating to each specialist, their notes, and Corbin's various surgeries. I held him while we waited for the blood test results to come back. Within the first hour, we had been told that regardless of the outcome, they would stabilise Corbin and send him down to Brisbane as they were much better equipped to handle such a complex case. When the doctor walked in and looked at me, I knew what the results had found—no words needed to be spoken.

I remember putting my finger to my lips behind Corbin's head to indicate not to say it out loud, and I mouthed the question: 'Liver?'

She nodded, biting her lip with sadness in her eyes. I nodded, and the resuscitation team, who had never left our side and were busy distracting Corbin with various DVD players and toys, kept up the act as I took the last bit of strength I had and said, without a hint of worry, 'Mummy needs to go to the bathroom quickly. Can you play with these lovely nurses and I will be right back?'

I slid out from underneath him and smiled. His little face smiled right back, none the wiser, and I walked through the curtains surrounding the bed and made it to the bathroom in time as I threw up and sobbed on my knees. My worst fear was coming true. It was happening; his liver was failing. *I can't save him. Again. I can't fix anything.*

I had absolutely no time to dwell on that. I splashed cold water on my face, scrubbed the vomit from my shirt with the paper towel, put a smile back on my face for Corbin's sake, and headed back out to the resuscitation unit to get ready to be transferred to Brisbane Children's Hospital.

Once again, it was the incredible health care system that saved my son's life. However, he turned an awful shade of yellow and was so weak from pain and medications that he was wheelchair-bound for a couple of weeks. His failing liver had ascending cholangitis, which is an infection that is often associated with his liver disease but is an incredibly painful and risky state to be in. It was a terrible, scary time, but he was able to pull through. During those moments, when I once again lay beside him in his hospital bed, I prayed I would do whatever it took to make everything better.

In the meantime, the wheels had well and truly fallen off the bus that we were trying to drive. I could no longer work as I needed to be by my son's side as he fought for life again. My husband had three children, including our not even two-month-old, that he needed to care for, and we were no longer able to pay any bills. It didn't matter how hard we worked; it wasn't going to fix this situation.

This was the very last time that I heard from my father. He sent me an email, and I opened it a week later as I sat beside my son in the hospital. This time, as my son clung to life, my newborn baby in my arms and my sons and husband desperately needing the little attention I was able to give them, I didn't reply to him. I have often questioned why I didn't. I tried to reach out a couple of years later but to no real response. It was clear that the decision I made that day to put my own little family first and survive, instead of allowing what I don't condone in my life anymore, was a forever decision. Some nights I can't sleep over it. Funny that—the guilt. My phone number has never changed; he just never called me again. I just kept swimming, treading water, and doing whatever it took to keep our family going.

So that is when the fire sale began. Corbin was released from the hospital in early October, the very same day as our first open home to sell our house. We prayed it would sell fast as we could no longer maintain mortgage repayments. That month, we sold Luke's boat, motorbike, project car, and anything else we could part with. By December, the price on our house had dropped due to housing developments that were being built around us. No-one wanted to buy an older property anymore. As each week went by and we got further and further into debt, we lost more and more hope.

Corbin was growing stronger each day, and by the time Christmas came, he had just started to walk and regain mobility again. The road to recovery was a long one for him this time. That year we had to accept a food hamper from Rhyz's high school for Christmas to get us through as we could no longer afford the bare necessities. They knew we were struggling as I had to call them in tears and explain I could not afford to pay his final term school fees when Corbin went into the hospital. Their kindness by remembering us at Christmas meant so much. We were so very alone in our grief. We still didn't qualify for government assistance as the sale of Luke's investment property was added as an income, even though we never physically saw a cent. So, we were left to continue to hold hands at night and stare at the ceiling and tell each other and the kids we would never give up, and we would find a way through it.

On New Year's Eve 2015, we got a call from the real estate agent to say that someone had finally made an offer on the house: $419,000. That was nearly $200,000 less than we were expecting. It was clearly the wrong time to sell, but we already had our backs against the wall and couldn't wait another second. Luke agreed to the price. Two thousand and fifteen was finally over. We had lost everything but each other, and we were determined that 2016 was going to be ours. We would rise together and regain the dignity that we lost and take our lives back on our terms for ourselves, by ourselves.

CHAPTER 16

I'LL BE MY OWN HOMECOMING QUEEN

The first week of 2016 was like something out of a *Choose Your Own Adventure* book. There were so many options we could take, but the risks had to be weighed carefully. I had to take leave from my position as a clinical coordinator and become a full-time carer to Corbin following his long recovery from his liver failure the few months prior. It was becoming really hard to juggle my career and his medical needs, so I knew I needed to find something that worked around our big family.

Following on from Luke's demotions that started to occur the previous year, the discussions between his family business had resulted in Luke's position no longer being made available to him. For the first time since he was fourteen years old, he no longer worked within his family's business that he had been an integral part of developing. He was devastated, and the betrayal he felt by being removed from his long-standing role was never to be repaired.

We had $54,000 in profit from the dismal sale of the family home, and we had combined debts of well over $70,000 and no assets left at all.

We knew we couldn't possibly afford to use that money to purchase another house with so much debt to our name. So, we took a deep breath and made one of the most daring decisions to date; we decided we would buy our own family business, one that would work around the needs of our family. We needed something that would keep the money coming in when we were in the hospital and hopefully, over time, allow us to pay off our enormous debts and finally start building a stable financial future for our family.

The first thing we knew was that it had to be a business that was in Luke's industry, of sorts. I would take over the reception, financial, and all other aspects of the company and we would work as a team.

Luke had one final purchase he wanted to make before handing over the control my way, and I had no idea what it was until he drove a replacement XP called Betty up the driveway and into my heart.

She was the most beautiful thing I had ever seen, and while she was going to need some work, she was stock standard, registered, and running a classic chrome bumper, and we were instantly in love. She was our spirit booster while we started piecing together our next steps.

With that lucky last, perfect purchase, we decided that all future financial decisions for the family household would become my responsibility as I was confident that I could help us crawl back from the situation we were in. So, sitting amongst packing boxes in our driveway on our first wedding anniversary, I gave Luke a leather-bound business book I told him we would use to write our hopes and dreams and goals in and we would tick them off as we went.

Little did we know the little brown book would soon hold the most inspiring story of a comeback that I could never have imagined. In January, we moved into a small rental property in Pelican Waters, and by February, we had found a business we thought might have potential in Kuluin, forty-five minutes from home. It was a run-down, old muffler shop that had been standing for more than twenty years. It was by no means flash, and the asking price was again way out of our league. As much as I was uncertain about the whole idea—I mean, I didn't even know what a muffler or an exhaust was at that stage—Luke was determined it was the right choice and approached the owner.

Luke offered a down payment that was a hefty chunk of what little money we were currently living off and struck up a deal to vendor-finance the remaining money owed for the following twelve months until the rest of the balance was paid off. Essentially, we paid a significant deposit, nearly everything we had, and then repaid the balance owing to the old owner over the next year; it was a scary notion.

We had nothing left to lose at this stage. We were determined to give it our all. If we failed, there would be no coming back: we would be bankrupt and financially ruined. But that wasn't the sort of people we were. We were going to make something of this, come hell or high water. And that is exactly what we did.

Two days before we opened the doors to our new venture, I made the heartbreaking call to sell my XP, Betty. I had no idea what type of overheads we were about to encounter, but I didn't want to start on the back foot. After two months with this beautiful car in my possession, I gritted my teeth and handed over the keys to the new owner and banked the money into the savings account for the business. To this day, this decision still haunts us, but we both know it was the smart one to make at the time. We had to put everything into this business if it had a chance, and we couldn't take any risks.

We walked into Kuluin Mufflers in March 2016 with well over $100,000 in debts and three of my four sons beside me in the lounge room we built beside the reception area because we couldn't even afford daycare. They were six months, eighteen months, and five years old; Rhyz was fifteen at the time.

I had never operated an accounting system in my life, and Luke had never used a pipe bender before that first day. But we had something we knew was going to blow the roof off; we were going to do whatever it took to make ourselves successful again. I stayed up late researching how to run various software; I started social media channels and held meetings with potential clients while I tube-fed my son in the other room. You know what? No-one saw that as unprofessional and not one person judged us.

I can't quite explain what happened next, as it evolved rapidly. It turned out that all those years of working hard for other people had in some way made me a natural in running my own business. I found a passion for marketing, and the sense of pride in working hard to piece our family's security back together drove me immensely. I rebranded our business, and within six weeks, we had to employ another full-time staff member to keep up with demand. Our sales within the first eight months went from $1,000 a week to $10,000, and it just exploded. We started producing our own systems under the 'KM'® brand and sold them throughout Australia and New Zealand online. I learnt to create our website with a lot of researching and launched our shop online. The online business soon started making as much money in a week as we used to within the workshop itself. We began to have orders come from overseas, and KM® exhausts started to pop up on social media, tagged in various parts of the country. It was quite surreal.

It was an incredible time for Luke and me. We had never expected to find this as our saving grace. We had hoped, and by gosh had we worked until we dropped to make it happen, but after a while, we realised we might have a fighting chance, and our future might not just be a pipe dream. Pardon the pun.

I then started realising what a huge community the car scene was, and I catered exclusively to them, with private open days and events that would see us sponsor them by giving away free systems and having a social outlet. They became not only friends, but like family. They saw what we were trying to do, and they cheered us on.

We realised how many people used their cars as a mental health outlet—a release, either by working on it or going for a cruise. I became a loud advocate for suicide prevention awareness and publicly announced that KM was a safe place to come if you needed help. You could sit back and watch us work on the rare and incredible builds, and if you needed company or professional help, we would give the details of support networks in the community. I started to be able to reach a wide circle of people that began to come in and ask for assistance with writing their resumes or enquiring about finding a job, so before long I added that to my area of expertise and started to help so many people. It felt incredible.

We wanted people, more than ever, to feel like they mattered and they were part of something. It worked. Everyone from teenagers to grown men would message and chat and come in and leave with a smile and say 'thank you'. We would go home each night feeling like we were going to be able to be more than just an exhaust shop. We were going to stand for something. We were going to bring hope and set an example.

After the open days, I started organising charity fundraisers to give back to the community who had supported us so much. The first was for Wishlist™. We held an old-school poker run that raised thousands towards incubators for the local hospitals that had been there time and time again for Corbin.

That evolved into an annual charity fundraising event; our most significant to date was called 'Weapon of Choice', where we took over an airfield usually filled with fighter jets and filled it with the most incredible cars ever seen. There were rare hot rods, old-school chrome-bumper cruisers, and everything in between. We turned it into a giant drive-in movie theatre that played *American Graffiti*, and a talented musician, Juzzie Smith, played in the hanger under a massive WWII plane to huge crowds who cheered the whole night. Once again, we raised over $10,000, and this time, it was for the wonderful charity Love Your Sister®, started by the inspiring Samuel Johnson. It was the most fulfilling thing I had ever done in my life.

The most wonderful part of days like these was the fact that people who had become family when I was younger and supported me until I was old enough to hold my own head above water were right there beside me. Mumma Jen and her youngest Beth (who became close friends with my Rhyz) would run the coffee van, and the amazing couple Gene and Mandy who had allowed me to live with them all those years ago when I had nowhere to turn had come back into my life and would come along supporting and cheering my achievements proudly. These people made it possible for me to give back; it was like a beautiful circle of karma—everyone helped everyone to make the impossible possible.

The business became an entity of its own, not only earning respect for the fabrication and design work of our exhaust systems, but for what we stood for in the community. We were the ultimate underdogs. We didn't fit in for one second in the corporate world, we just wanted our family together and to one day own that piece of land with a small cottage that our children's children could call home. We were getting there; we worked long hours—up early and home late—but we did it all together. The kids were with us side by side, and we got to celebrate the victories one by one as we ticked off the goals we set out in our little leather book.

I then decided to launch a coffee van and create our brand of cold-press KM® coffee we serve at our exclusive events. It was a massive hit, and the retro-style van that was built to look like an old 'woody' surfer wagon went down well with the coastal car scene. I wanted to experiment with some ideas I had, so I started to design a clothing range. When our first shirts sold out within twenty-four hours, I knew I was onto something. It has never slowed down. The creativity and freedom my business gives me have been blessings I could never have imagined.

It did, however, take its toll physically to grow that fast. In that first year when I was taking the three children to work with me every day and was learning how to manage it all, my body physically fell apart from the load, and I ended up in hospital burnt out and with crippling chest pain, struggling to breathe. I was discharged and told to rest up, but with no-one but each other to rely on, I was certainly not about to let anyone down and was back at work the next day. We had to push hard, working long hours until breaking point to get ourselves into the position we needed to be in, and I was prepared to do anything to help our family achieve those goals.

In 2017, quite unexpectedly, I won a local Young Business Woman of the Year award when I had no idea that anyone in the business world would ever take me seriously. I was one of the only tattooed people in the room, and when I walked into the fancy room that evening, I stood out from the hundreds of others. I was so sure I had no chance of winning that I was helping to run a supercar fundraising function that was downstairs the same night.

I had planned to clap politely when someone else won my section and then sneak out and play with the supercars downstairs. I had spent the previous few months assisting with the event, which was raising money for local foster children. When they announced the winner and my name was called, I was shaking. After I received my trophy, I stood on stage, delivering my speech to a packed room about where I had started and how I had built my business and why. As I began to finish the last sentence, I watched as every person in the room stood and cheered loudly and gave me a standing ovation. It was the most surreal moment of my life. The most ironic part of that evening—and I mentioned it in my speech—was how that was the same room that the blue light school discos were held all those decades ago. I was standing in literally the same room that my husband and I had shared our first kiss. It was a wonderful moment for our family, and a time to celebrate what we had accomplished.

I had never attended a networking event in my life before that evening and didn't quite understand what was coming next, but sure enough, it came with a bang, and it has never slowed since. Then the social media attention started. I have lost count of the television interviews, magazines, newspaper stories, and radio chats I have had, each time I still pinch myself. I am still the same plain girl who most days wears leggings as pants to work with at least one child attached to her hip and juggling all the balls in the air at once.

I have since done major speaking events in front of hundreds of people. My confidence has grown each time, and I no longer shake when I stand on stage and share my story or encourage business owners to achieve their goals.

I have refused to attend events I feel aren't part of something I would like to be associated with, and I am certainly not part of anything that hides behind the premise of supporting others when the reality is very different.

I just don't do fake well. I am incredibly confident in the woman I am. It may have taken me years to get here, but I like myself, and I know there is so much competition out there that I do not want to be part of negativity in any way. There seems to be a lot of jealousy involved in this award-winning arena, and I have seen grown woman crying and having tantrums while all dressed in their finery because they didn't win a category. It is terrible sportsmanship and lacks class. People need to understand that winning or losing a competition or an award does not define them. They won't be any less or any better a businessperson because of the outcome. It is undoubtedly a rewarding experience to take part in, and I have met some beautiful people along the way and made some wonderful friends.

More than half of what I do for the community and charity work is not known to the public, and I would be upset if it was. It takes away the entire purpose of doing it, and sometimes the people I am helping are in delicate situations. It would be inappropriate and undignified to expose them.

I think certain things need to be kept silent to retain the meaning of the sentiment. However, being asked to be a guest speaker for the Salvation Army's Red Shield Appeal to talk about how they once assisted poor, pregnant, teenage Angie has undoubtedly been one of the great highlights. When I was asked to be the guest speaker at the Salvation Army's Red Shield Appeal, it was a really emotional moment for me. I stood in front of hundreds of people from our community and opened up about how I was once a scared pregnant teenager who relied on the kindness and support of The Salvation Army. I spoke about how I used to await their visits to my run-down house and how their food boxes kept me going. I explained to everyone that although I was now successful and no longer needed a helping hand, the memory of their assistance never left me through the years. I reiterated how far I had come in the past couple of decades and the flow-on effect was alive and well with me now assisting others just like they had done to me all that time ago. I felt that I had come full circle.

I tend to keep the blinkers on, as I have from day one. I stay in my lane and focus on my own race. It has worked incredibly well so far, and each year has seen significant growth from the year prior. Being involved in every aspect of the business has contributed to its success, without a doubt. Running all the financials myself means that at any time I know exactly how we are sitting financially. Marketing-wise, being the person who controls the social media channels means I have a direct connection to our customer base. I know their feedback and what is hot in the market right now. If I outsourced any of those parts of my business, I don't think I would have the ability to continue to think outside the box when it comes to standing out with our various marketing procedures and events. It allows me to be creative and authentic in my approach to business. When I say Kuluin Mufflers is part of me, it most certainly is an extension of my personality. It allows me to reach out to the community and give back. We began hosting an annual toy run every Christmas and supplied toys to the local hospitals, and then we expanded to gift presents to the Sunshine Coast foster families as well. Suddenly, if anyone needed some help, they knew they could reach out and I would try my best to make it happen. I began to mentor local kids, and the satisfaction of being able to just be available for someone who needs a friendly ear or some guidance has made everything feel like it has fallen into place. Suddenly, the girl who didn't have anywhere to turn when she was younger is now able to be there for others so that they don't feel that sense of loneliness that I did all those years ago.

I do have a tendency to—as my husband likes to say—'light wildfires' and I don't mean to do it; it just happens so fast. One moment someone reaches out for some assistance, and the next minute I am closing down the main road and hiring a stage, and a musician to play to raise money for those in need. It always starts small but tends to burn into this brilliant wildfire that lights the way for so many people to feel the warmth. It is the most satisfying part of my life. Watching folks join us and assist others through the platform of our business is something that brings me so much joy and pride.

The 2017 Sunshine Coast Business Awards then announced it was presenting us with the award for Excellence in Social Responsibility, and it was such a privilege to be recognised for a contribution that I believe to be so important to the community. This award had so much meaning to us, and we were chuffed to have this honour in our name. I do feel it's an essential role of local businesses to use their public platform and encourage others to support the community around them.

It was not long after this that I decided I wanted to start my own registered and legally recognised charity funded exclusively by the profits of my business, and that had no administration fees or costs deducted from the funds raised. All the fundraising money would go directly to families on the Sunshine Coast who struggled financially due to having a chronically or terminally ill child. I never wanted what happened to us to happen to someone else. I wanted to create something so a parent would not have to choose between going to work to pay the bills or being by their sick child's bedside. I wanted a charity that existed to cover medical costs, household bills, and mortgage repayments that were late due to the pressures of juggling a terminally ill child. My proudest moment to date would be launching Driven By KM into the community in July 2018. It is run entirely by volunteers; not a single cent is paid to any board members, workers, events, etc. and Kuluin Mufflers covers all administration costs.

Of course, the directors of this charity had to be people I trust, so it was a no-brainer to have the seats filled by dear friends closest to me to form a crucial part of the board of directors. My closest friend Leah, who has been like a sister to me for years, she was the very first person I asked to join me in building the charity into what it is today. Matt went through primary and high school with me (and was there with Sam and Luke after Rhyz was born); his wonderful wife and dear friend of mine, Kimberley, filled a seat. Sam's wife Trina, who is like family to me, also plays a large role as a director. These friends have stood by my side for decades, and I couldn't imagine doing something so significant without them, they sit proudly among the other incredible directors; Ryan, Paul and Darren who all play a significant and important role in creating a charity that offers assistance and hope to so many in need. We have been able to assist families who are going through their darkest days by stepping in and covering any financial concern they have. It is a very humbling role, and our board of directors and committee members are very proud of ourselves for what we have created.

It is recognised as an official registered charity within Australia, and we are so grateful for the support and generous donations we have received by the community. I may not have known how to do any of the official work associated with running a charity before I started one, but I had no idea how to run a business before I owned one, either. I just knew it was pivotal support the community was lacking, so I felt it was crucial to make it happen, and I was so proud when it came to fruition.

In March 2019, I was given the ultimate privilege of winning Telstra's Business Women's Award for Queensland in the 'Small Business' category. I could barely believe what was happening as the gorgeous Tracey Spicer congratulated me, and once again, cameras rolled as I made my acceptance speech. It was the most magnificent surprise as Telstra's awards are renowned for being judged on merit, therefore are held in high regard. You need to provide actual hard copy financial proof that you are as successful as you are claiming to be. This award was special to me as it wasn't a popularity contest. Every single person in that room was a true professional and shone in their area of expertise. I am so proud to be part of the exclusive alumni that show great support to one another.

This launched me into an entirely different level of opportunities and the ability to meet some idols due to the incredible support of the Business Chicks Network that works closely nurturing business-women like myself. They invited me to attend and meet Ita Buttrose, who is an Australia icon in so many ways for her pure hard work, professionalism, and the way she set about shattering the glass ceilings years prior in order for us ladies to keep standing up and being seen. I must admit, I got the giggles when we were introduced. Celebrities, in general, don't make me nervous, but those people whose intelligence and pure classiness are at Ita's level definitely had me grinning broadly. What a wonderful woman.

With Telstra and Business Chicks supporting my career, I was placed in rooms with other passionate ladies who were also making an impact, not only in the career world but in their surrounding communities. This gave me a chance to make connections and really find the support network that helped propel me forward with confidence, knowing I was on the right path. I was even named as one of four finalists for The Australian of the Year Local Community Hero in recognition for what I did to help those around me and in the community. It was an immeasurable honour to be acknowledged in such a high regard and I cried when the QLD Premier's office called to notify me of the award.

I began being asked to give motivational speeches at business events and to talk to other teenage mothers about how I was able to find my feet again. To break that barrier down and let people see that behind great success there are failures and low points, I think it makes people believe that they are capable of anything, too. That is incredibly satisfying for me, as I wished I had someone tell me when I was younger not to be defined by my circumstances at that time. I think it would have assisted me in holding my head higher when I needed to. Now I hope that people see that when I talk to them that they too can come from nothing and be able to not only support their family but also help other people around them.

I would never have reached that level of success without my husband, Luke. We have done this together, the whole way; it was a team effort, and his workmanship and dedication to continually lift our game has allowed me to shine in my area of the business as well. We have three hoists that run full-time now, a team of five staff members, and we are often booked out up to six weeks in advance. We have people travel from other states to get work done, and our business prides itself on its reputation. It has been a long couple of years to reach the peak we have now, and we are only just warming up. We are so proud of all we have accomplished. We were desperate to find a way to put food on the table for our children and dig our way out of our mammoth debt only a few years ago. Together we have created something that not only supports our family but so many others in the community around us. We have grown more in love as each day has passed and still cannot believe we have the privilege of growing old together with such a beautiful family. Some days I do pinch myself as to how I got so lucky.

Where am I now, you ask? Well, let's end this on the highest point to date. In June 2019, I made the final payment that enabled Luke, me, and our family to be entirely debt-free. All those years of holding our breath, not knowing how we would make ends meet or how we would climb out from the overwhelming debt, were finally behind us. In three and a half years, we had paid off approximately $159,000 in total, which includes the vendor finance payments on the business (less the deposit). That feeling was irreplaceable. I have a thriving business, the ongoing ability to provide for my family throughout my son's continuing surgeries, and hope. Finally, all those years of around-the-clock work had started to pay off. The option of buying our own home is now within reach, and I am sure when that day comes, I will be an emotional mess.

Our business is booming and has gone from strength to strength without missing a beat each year, and we now have a huge team of incredible employees in place that assists us in our expansion. International and Australian sales have far exceeded what we could have ever imagined, and I am so grateful to have built this company with my husband side by side. Kuluin Mufflers will always be a business that provides not only for our family but offers considerable support for the community where we live.

The charity that I run, Driven By KM, offers financial support to those with terminally and chronically ill children, so I kept my promise there to whoever it was upstairs that I used to pray to in order to save my son in those dark hours. I feel that continuing to help everyone around me might—just maybe—buy me a little more time with Corbin, and I am sure trying my darndest to help everyone whose path crosses mine.

I try so hard that sometimes I am almost broken by the strain, but I feel that I can't jinx anything, in case I lose my son. It is a horrible gut-wrenching pull of knowing that forever I have promised to do so much in order to have my son's health. *What if I can't be successful in saving someone else's plight? Will my son suffer?* It torments me, and although I personally get so much satisfaction within my soul from being able to be there for another struggling family, I still worry if one day whoever is upstairs might decide it is no longer enough. Talk about taking mother's guilt to a new level!

I have an online blog that reaches around the world and allows me to share my journey with others and show everyone what happens behind all the smoke and mirrors. It also stops me chattering my husband's ear off all evening long as it gives me a great creative outlet.

I am surrounded by the most supportive group of friends; some the same ones I grew up with, and some I have met along the way. I am fortunate to live my life with such beautiful humans by my side. Our family regularly gathers around the dining tables of friends and goes on Sunday car rides for coffee and cake. My heart is filled with friends who have more than compensated for any void my family may have left all those years ago. We have become an extended support group to one another, and I consider them my family in every way. I am not sure they will ever know how much they mean to me, but I sure as heck am grateful for them being in my life.

Rhyz completed high school a year earlier due to his outstanding academic record. He grew up to be a strapping six-foot-tall, charismatic gentleman with a broad smile, a passion for helping others, and a work ethic that rivals most. He is a brilliant and funny human and very much my best friend. We have an unshakeable bond, and I burst with pride whenever I speak of him. The moment he turned eighteen, he legally changed his surname to the one he'd known since the age of ten: Ben's surname. It was a huge deal as he was now formally his father's son. It was touching for everyone.

Corbin has just had his 27th surgery (I think, I have run out of fingers and toes to count on) and is stable. He is under the care of the liver transplant team but is not currently on the transplant list. That liver, while trying to scare us at times, is still holding strong, as is our hope. We haven't gone twelve months without surgery yet, but he lives a happy life without too much pain. He is even able to attend school with his brothers when he is well enough. The rest of the time, he just joins me at the business in the lounge room next to the office, or I will work from home when he needs to rest. He has a tutor to assist with his learning, and he loves swimming in the ocean more than anything in the world. Corbin continues to be a light that gives hope to everyone he meets. He is an undefinable miracle and, like all his brothers, provides us with a reason to live.

Dash is a great ball of energy who lives up to his name—a full-speed bolt of lightning. Always quick to laugh, he loves nothing more than reading and riding his bike. He is a perfectionist and an outdoor soul who has bright eyes and a smile that makes you instantly warm to him. He is a brilliantly enthusiastic student and is quick to make friends anywhere we go. He brightens my days with his caring nature, although I do have to chase him for hugs.

The baby of the family, Ace Danger, is a sweet little ball of attitude with a contagious laugh, an obsession with hedgehogs, and a need to be snuggled close to me at all times. He is stubborn—more than the other kids, but has a hilarious knack for comic timing that often finds the household doubling over in laughter with his quick wit. Ace is softly spoken but unrelenting in his tantrums. When he shines his charismatic smile and sparkly eyes in your direction, all is forgiven. He is like my little shadow, and he and Dash are inseparable.

My sons are the highlight of my life, the fundamental reason I live and breathe; they brighten my world and fill my heart and home with happiness far beyond anything I ever imagined. For all those years, when I didn't have my own home or family, the life I live now far exceeds any dreams or expectations I had. I am happily married to the true love of my life, who continues to be the most incredible man all our children adore and admire. I am the luckiest lady in the world. He is my best friend, the person who I imagine growing old with and filling our lives with memories that we make together. Our love is timeless; it is something that I shall be grateful for until the end of my days. He makes me feel like I matter every single day of my life. I can barely put into words the devotion I have for him.

In June 2019, when I paid the last repayment, making us debt-free, I was able to purchase a brand-new car for the first time in my life. I had spent the previous few years arriving at these glamourous awards nights parking next to Maseratis and Lexuses in an old beat-up Honda Civic with a window that wouldn't close properly. It had a permanent stench of wet towel and a bumper that was held together with zip ties. It had never bothered Luke and me, and I would always giggle as we would pull into cocktail events in our ballgown and tux and step out of our leaky, but loveable trusty Civic. It was time to step it up. It had been years of pure back-breaking work, and we had done it.

When the salesman, Darren, called me to let me know that my Ram Laramie® truck was ready to collect and was featuring a big fancy bow on top with all the mods and extras, I broke down in tears on the phone, as did he. He knew what we had been through and he was privy to what we were about to do with the truck's maiden voyage.

First, we drove to the school and picked up all our children mid-way through class and revelled in seeing their little eyes widen as big as saucers when we showed them what I had just bought. Then we drove for hours to have a picnic in the park with my dear friend

Leah and ate ice creams as we stared at the truck in awe. Leah gave me the greatest gift when she had her first daughter: choosing me to be her godmother and honorary aunty. I officially had a niece and more family to call my own. The real excitement about purchasing this truck was about to be undertaken within a week of its collection, as we packed it up and with the three boys strapped across the back seat, we headed to New South Wales for a very special day in our family's history.

Once we arrived, our beautiful blended family, including Ben and his beautiful soulmate and wife, Jane, walked into the Army barracks. Shaking with overwhelming pride and sheer joy, together, our family cried, cheered, and celebrated as we watched Rhyz march out from the Australian Army with his rifle-green beret as a proud infantry soldier.

The young boy I had devoted my life to had achieved the dream he had worked so hard to reach himself. Watching him succeed and be so satisfied and happy in life gave me a joy that is beyond compare. As I sat there next to my husband—my best friend and the man who has loved me for over two decades and without who I would be lost—the feeling that life had just begun for us and we could take the foot off the pedal and enjoy these moments sunk in. We had ridden out the most challenging times together without missing a beat. Family is our most important asset and what makes our everyday life worth living. We had also accomplished what the generation before me didn't: we kept our family together despite a divorce. Our children never grew up separated from their parents, and in return, we all get the pleasure of celebrating such memorable milestones proudly together.

Our children never have to think twice about who they share their special moments with; they know that both sets of parents and in-laws will all jump in together and fill a pew at high school graduation or share a table for birthday parties, cheering the whole way.

Luke and I watch on as Ben and Jane don't hesitate to reach out and extend hugs to Dash and Ace, as the boys have grown up knowing all about how wonderful Corbin's dad and step-mum are, and are so excited each time we all get together. It makes life so much nicer for everyone involved. Everyone's role is important, and while I don't doubt for a second there are moments when we—out of view of the children—roll our eyes at each other, we know we are blessed to have what we do, and we are grateful for every moment we get to share.

Being a devoted mother and wife has been the greatest role I have ever had the privilege of fulfilling. Nothing comes close. It may not always have been easy but, by gosh, the view from the top right now, surrounded by the happy faces of my sons and my loving husband, makes every hard step worthwhile.

I may not have come from much, but I am certainly well on my way to creating a legacy my children can be proud of and that can give them the confidence to reach their full potential as well. They will know every step of the way that my love is unconditional, they are worthy, and they are loved beyond explanation.

Jaqueline Onassis once said: 'If you bungle raising children, I don't think whatever else you do matters very much.'

I couldn't have said it better myself.

ABOUT THE AUTHOR

Angie Mansey is the proud (depending on if they are behaving on the day) mother of four rather energetic sons and is married to her best friend, Luke, who has been listening to her incessant chatter since 1996. A full-time carer to one son and a laundry slave to all four (five, if hubby is included), Angie is an award-winning business-woman, confident public speaker, and philanthropist with various causes close to her heart. Angie is also the founder and director of Driven By KM, a charity that provides financial support to the families of terminally and chronically ill children on the Sunshine Coast. An enthusiastic believer that a cup of tea fixes most things, and an outstanding ability to remember '90s music lyrics but never can recall which way is east, Angie is also fluent in sarcasm and positivity.

ACKNOWLEDGMENTS

Thank you to the team who helped me to create the perfect book cover image; Hair and photography by the insanely talented Renae-Soppe-Bryan from Sunshine Coast Pinup School.

Makeup by the ultimate dream team (and my nearest and dearest friends) Emily Cox and Heather Smith Maclean from Tan Addiction Beauty Bar Caloundra.

Wardrobe courtesy of my kind hearted friend Lee-Anne Maker-Evans via Kitten D'Amour who drove hours in a storm to make my entire fairy-tale come to life. A million thank yous for being the wonderful person you are.

Thank you to my husband, my true 'ride or die' and my soulmate who is constantly encouraging of the wild fires I may start even though I am sure I have given him a twitch with the ferocity of them over the years. We've got this.

To my Leah, thank you for being my best friend. There is no one I would rather eat cob loaf with at 2 am in my pjs. You make my world brighter just by being in it.

To Ali, your support and confidence in getting this book from an idea into reality was a game changer, thank you for your friendship.

Vas, you changed the playing field for my family and gave us a real shot when the odds weren't in our favour. You have been a true friend over the years and I am grateful for your friendship.

Facebook Blog: https://www.facebook.com/angiemansey
Instagram: https://www.instagram.com/angie_mansey
Linkedin: https://www.linkedin.com/in/angelamansey
Driven By KM: https://www.drivenbykm.com/
Kuluin Mufflers: https://www.kuluinmufflers.com.au

Awards:

2021   Australian of the Year Queensland Local Hero Nominee

2020   Sunshine Coast Citizen of the Year Finalist

2019   Telstra Business Women's Awards Queensland Small Business Winner

2017   Sunshine Coast Business Awards Excellence in Social Responsibility

2017   Sunshine Coast Business Women's Network Young Businesswoman of the Year

ENDNOTES

1   *About Hyperemesis Gravidarum,* Hyperemesis Gravidarum Australia. Retrieved from https://www.hyperemesisaustralia.org.au/about-hg September 3, 2020.

2   *Toxaemia of pregnancy (pre-eclampsia).* MyDr.com.au Retrieved from https://www.mydr.com.au/babies-pregnancy/toxaemia-of-pregnancy on October 12, 2020

3   *Pediatric Tracheoesophageal Fistula and Esophageal Atresia,* Children's National. Retrieved from https://childrensnational.org/visit/conditions-and-treatments/genetic-disorders-and-birth-defects/tracheoesophageal-fistula-and-esophageal-atresia October 12, 2020.

4   *VACTERL Association,* National Centre for Advancing Translational Sciences. Retrieved from https://rarediseases.info.nih.gov/diseases/5443/vacterl-association September 3, 2020.

5   *Kasai Procedure,* University of California San Francisco Department of Surgery. Retrieved from https://surgery.ucsf.edu/conditions--procedures/kasai-procedure.aspx September 3, 2020.